IN DEFENSE OF HOUSING

IN DEFENSE
OF HOUSING

The Politics of Crisis

DAVID MADDEN
PETER MARCUSE

VERSO
London • New York

First published by Verso 2016
© David Madden and Peter Marcuse, 2016

3 5 7 9 10 8 6 4 2

Verso
UK: 6 Meard Street, London W1F 0EG
US: 20 Jay Street, Suite 1010, Brooklyn, NY 11201
versobooks.com

Verso is the imprint of New Left Books

ISBN-13: 978-1-78478-354-9 (PB)
ISBN-13: 978-1-78478-353-2 (HB)
ISBN-13: 978-1-78478-356-3 (US EBK)
ISBN-13: 978-1-78478-355-6 (UK EBK)

British Library Cataloguing in Publication Data
A catalogue record for this book is available from the British Library

Library of Congress Cataloging-in-Publication Data
A catalog record for this book is available from the Library of Congress

Typeset in Fournier by Hewer Text UK Ltd, Edinburgh
Printed in the UK by CPI Group (UK) Ltd, Coydon CR0 4YY

Contents

Acknowledgments

We would like to thank the team at Verso for helping us produce this book, and especially Leo Hollis, whose advice and steady encouragement helped us make the text more lucid and readable. We warmly acknowledge the support of the many colleagues and friends who, through close reading or insightful conversation, helped us improve this book. We are grateful to Neil Brenner for giving us input and encouragement. Jenny Robinson provided helpful feedback on an earlier version of this project. Michelle Rosales provided research assistance early in our collaboration. We thank Desiree Fields, Tom Waters, and the participants in the Wohnungsfrage Academy in Berlin, 2015, for reading and discussing versions of these chapters. And we want to acknowledge all of the friends, colleagues, students, and activists who helped us develop these arguments, especially the people involved with the housing and rent control movements in New York, including the Planners Network, the National Lawyers Guild, various organizations of public housing tenants, Picture the Homeless, Community Voices Heard, FUREE, and many other organizations too many to list.

Some parts of this book include material previously published by Peter Marcuse. Chapter two draws on "Residential Alienation, Home Ownership and the Limits of Shelter Policy," *Journal of Sociology and Social Welfare* 3.2 (1975): 181–203. Chapter three includes sections of "The Other Side of Housing: Oppression and Liberation," *Scandinavian Housing and Planning Research* 4.Sup1 (1987): 232–70. Chapter four is an updated and rewritten version of "Housing Policy and the Myth of the Benevolent State," pp. 248–63 in Rachel G. Bratt, Chester Hartman, and Ann Meyerson, eds, *Critical Perspectives on Housing* (Philadelphia: Temple University Press, 1986). Chapter five incorporates sections of "Housing Movements in the USA," *Housing, Theory and Society* 16.2 (1999): 67–86.

Finally, Peter would like to thank his wife for love, affection, and tolerance over more than twice the twenty-five-year span during which the above-mentioned pieces were written. And he wants to thank the numerous colleagues, activists, and activist organizations listed above with which he has been involved and from whom he has learned most of what is contained here. David would like to thank his family, colleagues, and friends for their care and encouragement. He thanks his colleagues at the LSE for their support, especially Suzi Hall and Fran Tonkiss. Emmanuelle Madden provided excellent company and welcome distraction through the writing and editing. David's greatest debt of thanks is to Rachel Faulkner-Gurstein, for her generous assistance and loving support.

Introduction

The Residential Is Political

The symptoms of housing crisis are everywhere in evidence today. Households are being squeezed by the cost of living. Homelessness is on the rise. Evictions and foreclosures are commonplace. Segregation and poverty, along with displacement and unaffordability, have become the hallmarks of today's cities. Urban and suburban neighborhoods are being transformed by speculative development, shaped by decisions made in boardrooms half a world away. Small towns and older industrial cities are struggling to survive.

In America, the housing crisis is especially acute in New York City. The city has more homeless residents now than at any time since the Great Depression. More than half of all households cannot afford the rent. Displacement, gentrification, and eviction are rampant.[1] Two pillars of New York's distinctive

---

1   Office of the Comptroller Scott Stringer, *The Growing Gap: New York City's Housing Affordability Challenge* (New York: Office of the Comptroller, 2014); Coalition for the Homeless, *New York City Homelessness: The Basic Facts* (New York: Coalition for the Homeless,

housing system—public housing and rent regulation—are both under threat.

But housing problems are not unique to New York. Shelter poverty is a problem throughout the United States.[2] According to the standard measures of affordability, there is no US state where a full-time minimum wage worker can afford to rent or own a one-bedroom dwelling. Nationwide, nearly half of all renting households spend an unsustainable amount of their income on rent, a figure that is only expected to rise. This is not only a big-city issue. Around 30 percent of rural households cannot afford their housing, including nearly half of all rural renters.[3]

2015); NYU Furman Center, *State of New York City's Housing and Neighborhoods in 2014* (New York: Furman Center, 2014), 38; Elvin Wyly, Kathe Newman, Alex Schafran, and Elizabeth Lee, "Displacing New York," *Environment and Planning A* 42.11 (2010): 2602–23.

2   Michael E. Stone, "Housing Affordability: One-Third of a Nation Shelter-Poor," pp. 38–60 in Rachel G. Bratt, Michael E. Stone, and Chester Hartman, eds, *A Right to Housing: Foundation for a New Social Agenda* (Philadelphia: Temple University Press, 2006). In their introduction, the editors note that in 2006, more than 100 million people across the United States were estimated to be living in "housing that is physically inadequate, in unsafe neighborhoods, over-crowded or way beyond what they can realistically afford." Rachel G. Bratt, Michael E. Stone, and Chester Hartman, "Why a Right to Housing Is Needed and Makes Sense: Editors' Introduction," pp. 1–19 in Bratt, Stone, and Hartman, *A Right to Housing*, 1.

3   National Low Income Housing Coalition, *Out of Reach 2015: Low Wages and High Rents Lock Renters Out* (Washington, DC: NLIHC, 2015), 1; Allison Charette, Chris Herbert, Andrew Jakabovics, Ellen Tracy Marya, and Daniel T. McCue, "Projecting Trends in Severely Cost-Burdened Renters: 2015–2025" (Enterprise Community Partners and Joint Center for Housing Studies, 2015), 6; Laurie

In fact, the housing crisis is global in scope. London, Shanghai, São Paulo, Mumbai, Lagos, indeed nearly every major city faces its own residential struggles. Land grabs, forced evictions, expulsions, and displacement are rampant. According to the United Nations, the homeless population across the planet may be anywhere between 100 million and one billion people, depending on how homelessness is defined. It has been estimated that globally there are currently 330 million households—more than a billion people—that are unable to find a decent or affordable home.[4] Some research suggests that in recent decades, residential displacement due to development, extraction, and construction has occurred on a scale that rivals displacement caused by disasters and armed conflicts. In China and India alone in the past fifty years, an estimated 100 million people have been displaced by development projects.[5]

Goodman, Rolf Pendall, and Jun Zhu, *Headship and Homeownership: What Does the Future Hold?* (Washington, DC: Urban Institute, 2015); Housing Assistance Council, *Taking Stock: Rural People, Poverty, and Housing in the 21st Century* (Washington, DC: HAC, 2012), 43–4.

4　Stefano Liberti, *Land Grabbing: Journeys in the New Colonialism*, trans. Enda Flannely (London: Verso, 2013); Saskia Sassen, *Expulsions: Brutality and Complexity in the Global Economy* (Cambridge, MA: Harvard University Press, 2014); United Nations Centre for Human Settlements, *An Urbanizing World: Global Report on Human Settlements* (UN-HABITAT, 1996), 6; McKinsey Global Institute, *A Blueprint for Addressing the Global Affordable Housing Challenge* (MGI, 2014), 2. It should be clear that the claim that the housing crisis is global does not imply that we are arguing that housing problems are identical everywhere.

5　Miloon Kothari, *The Global Crisis of Displacement and Evictions: A Housing and Land Rights Perspective* (New York: Rosa Luxemburg Stiftung, 2015), 6.

And yet if there is broad recognition of the existence of a housing crisis, there is no deep understanding of why it occurs, much less what to do about it. The dominant view today is that if the housing system is broken, it is a temporary crisis that can be resolved through targeted, isolated measures. In mainstream debates, housing tends to be understood in narrow terms. The provision of adequate housing is seen as a technical problem and technocratic means are sought to solve it: better construction technology, smarter physical planning, new techniques for management, more homeownership, different zoning laws, and fewer land use regulations. Housing is seen as the domain of experts like developers, architects, or economists. Certainly, technical improvements in the housing system are possible, and some are much needed. But the crisis is deeper than that.

We see housing in a wider perspective: as a political-economic problem. The residential is political—which is to say that the shape of the housing system is always the outcome of struggles between different groups and classes. Housing necessarily raises questions about state action and the broader economic system. But the ways in which social antagonisms shape housing are too often obscured. This book is an attempt to bring them to light.

Housing is under attack today. It is caught within a number of simultaneous social conflicts. Most immediately, there is a conflict between housing as lived, social space and housing as an instrument for profitmaking—a conflict between housing as *home* and as *real estate*. More broadly, housing is the subject of contestation between different ideologies, economic interests, and political projects. More broadly still, the housing crisis stems from the inequalities and antagonisms of class society.

Many of the examples here are drawn from housing struggles in the city that we know best, New York City.[6] But our target is much broader: the role of housing within contemporary society, economy, and politics. Housing inevitably raises issues about power, inequality, and justice in capitalist society. Much of this book is thus about helping to recover a language through which to understand housing conflicts and to contest residential injustice. We want to refocus the debate around political-economic processes like commodification, alienation, exploitation, oppression, and liberation. And we seek to develop a critical understanding of the actors and forces that have produced the housing system in the past and the present.

Reposing the Housing Question

The classic statement on the political-economic aspects of housing was written by Friedrich Engels in 1872. At the time, few disputed the fact that housing conditions for the industrial proletariat were unbearable. What Engels called "the housing question" was the question of why working-class housing appeared in the condition as it did, and what should be done about it.[7]

---

6   We recognize that our analysis becomes more limited the farther away it moves from contexts like New York. And we are not claiming that housing is alike in all North American or Western European cities, nor that housing problems in these places are identical to residential issues in other regions. But we do seek to draw connections where appropriate. And we hope that, where relevant, our points can be applied to other contexts.

7   Frederick [*sic*] Engels, *The Housing Question*, ed. C. P. Dutt (London: Lawrence and Wishart, 1936 [1872]).

Engels was generally pessimistic about the prospects for housing struggles per se. Criticizing bourgeois attempts at housing reform, he argued that housing problems should be understood as some of "the numerous, *smaller*, secondary evils which result from the present-day capitalist mode of production."[8] He concluded, "As long as the capitalist mode of production continues to exist, it is folly to hope for an isolated solution to the housing question or of any other social question affecting the fate of the workers."[9] For Engels, housing struggles were derivative of class struggle. Housing problems, then, could only be addressed through social revolution.

We take from Engels the idea that the housing question is embedded within the structures of class society. Posing the housing question today means uncovering the connections between societal power and the residential experience. It means asking who and what housing is for, who controls it, who it empowers, who it oppresses. It means questioning the function of housing within globalized neoliberal capitalism.[10]

However, residential struggles today are not simply derivative of other conflicts. Housing movements are significant political actors in their own right. The housing question may not be resolvable under capitalism. But the shape of the housing system can be acted upon, modified, and changed.

---

8   Ibid., 18, emphasis in original.

9   Ibid., 73.

10   On conceptualizing neoliberalism, see William Davies, *The Limits of Neoliberalism: Authority, Sovereignty and the Logic of Competition* (London: SAGE, 2014); Jamie Peck, *Constructions of Neoliberal Reason* (Oxford: Oxford University Press, 2013); David Harvey, *A Brief History of Neoliberalism* (Oxford: Oxford University Press, 2007); Neil Brenner and Nik Theodore, eds, *Spaces of Neoliberalism: Urban Restructuring in North America and Western Europe* (Oxford: Blackwell, 2002).

The social theorist Henri Lefebvre helps us understand the political role of housing and the potential for changing it. In his 1968 book *The Right to the City*, Lefebvre argued that industrial insurrection was not the only force for social transformation. An "urban strategy" for revolutionizing society was possible.[11] Given changes to the nature of work and of urban development, the industrial proletariat was no longer the only agent of revolutionary change, or even the predominant one. Lefebvre claimed that there was a new political subject: the city dweller. More generally, Lefebvre invokes the politics of "the inhabitant," a category that includes any worker, in the broadest sense, seen from the perspective of everyday social and residential life.[12]

Lefebvre is vague about what exactly the inhabitant as a political subject will accomplish with the urban revolution. But he does point to a different way of inhabiting. He imagines a future where social needs would not be subordinated to economic necessity, where disalienated dwelling space would be

---

11   "The Right to the City", pp. 63–181 in Henri Lefebvre, *Writings on Cities*, ed. and trans. Eleonore Kofman and Elizabeth Lebas (Malden, MA: Blackwell, 1996 [1967]), 154. And see Lefebvre, *The Urban Revolution*, trans. Robert Bononno (Minneapolis, MN: University of Minnesota Press, 2003 [1970]). See also Peter Marcuse, "Reading the Right to the City," *City* 18.1 (2014), 4–9; Marcuse, "From Critical Urban Theory to the Right to the City," *City* 13.2–3 (2009), 185–97; David J. Madden, "City Becoming World: Nancy, Lefebvre, and the Global–Urban Imagination," *Environment and Planning D* 30.5 (2012), 772–87.

12   Lefebvre, "Right to the City," 159. On the idea of the "politics of the inhabitant," see Mark Purcell, "Excavating Lefebvre: The Right to the City and Its Urban Politics of the Inhabitant," *GeoJournal* 58 (2002), 99–108.

universally available, where both equality and difference would be the basic principles of social and political life.[13]

Whether or not anything like Lefebvre's urban revolution is on the horizon, we can use his ideas to understand a basic point: the politics of housing involve a bigger set of actors and interests than is recognized either by mainstream debates or by conventional political-economic analyses such as that offered by Engels. In the orthodox account, the only conflicts that matter are those surrounding exploitation and value. But the ruling class also needs to solidify its rule, and preserving the ability to exploit is only one aspect of this. There are also political, social, and ideological imperatives that significantly affect residential conditions.

In the financialized global economy—which was only beginning to emerge when Lefebvre was writing—real estate has come to have new prominence in relation to industrial capital. Housing and urban development today are not secondary phenomena. Rather, they are becoming some of the main processes driving contemporary global capitalism. If Lefebvre

---

13   Lefebvre describes this world using the word "urban," but with his idiosyncratic usage of the term: "The *right to the city* cannot be conceived of as a simple visiting right or as a return to traditional cities. It can only be formulated as a transformed and renewed *right to urban life*. It does not matter whether the urban fabric encloses the countryside and what survives of peasant life, as long as the 'urban,' place of encounter, priority of use value, inscription in space of a time promoted to the rank of a supreme resource among all resources, finds its morphological base and its practico-material realization" (Lefebvre, "Right to the City," 158, emphasis in original). Lefebvre is not talking about any actual city so much as articulating a theory of urbanization and what he sees as its political potential.

is right, housing is becoming an ever more important site for the reproduction of the system—a change that might open new strategic possibilities for housing movements to achieve social change.

Whose Crisis?

Critics, reformers, and activists have invoked the term "housing crisis" for more than a hundred years. The phrase once again became pervasive after the global economic meltdown of 2008. But we need to be careful with this usage of the concept of crisis.

The idea of crisis implies that inadequate or unaffordable housing is abnormal, a temporary departure from a well-functioning standard. But for working-class and poor communities, housing crisis is the norm.[14] Insufficient housing has been the mark of dominated groups throughout history. Engels made exactly this point:

> The so-called housing shortage, which plays such a great role in the press nowadays, does not consist in the fact that the working class generally lives in bad, overcrowded or unhealthy dwellings. *This* shortage is not something peculiar to the present; it is not even one of the sufferings peculiar to the modern proletariat in contradistinction to all earlier oppressed classes. On the contrary, all oppressed

---

14　See Peter Marcuse and W. Dennis Keating, "The Permanent Housing Crisis: The Failures of Conservatism and the Limitations of Liberalism," pp. 139–62 in Bratt, Stone, and Hartman, *A Right to Housing*.

classes in all periods suffered more or less uniformly from it.[15]

For the oppressed, housing is always in crisis. The reappearance of the term "housing crisis" in headlines represents the experiences of middle-class homeowners and investors, who faced unexpected residential instability following the 2008 financial implosion.

The idea of a housing crisis is politically loaded. Though the concept of crisis has a long history in critical theory and radical practice, it can be deployed for other purposes. In the United States, the discourse of housing crisis is often used to condemn state "interference" in housing markets. In the UK, the crisis frame is invoked in support of granting new legal powers to developers in order to override local planning guidelines.

Discrete moments when housing crises become acute tend to be interpreted away as exceptions to a fundamentally sound system. But this is an ideological distortion. The experience of crisis in the residential sphere reflects and amplifies the broader tendencies towards insecurity in capitalist societies. Housing crisis is a predictable, consistent outcome of a basic characteristic of capitalist spatial development: housing is not produced and distributed for the purposes of dwelling for all; it is produced and distributed as a commodity to enrich the few. Housing crisis is not a result of the system breaking down but of the system working as it is intended.[16]

---

15   Engels, *The Housing Question*, 17, emphasis in original.

16   Cf. "homelessness exists not because the system is failing to work as it should, but because the system *is* working as it must," from Peter Marcuse, "Neutralizing Homelessness," *Socialist Review* 88.1 (1988), 93.

We should reject ideological versions of the concept of housing crisis. But the term is still useful. For those compelled to dwell in oppressive and alienating conditions, housing crisis is not empty rhetoric; it is daily reality. To millions of households, "crisis" describes precisely the chaos, fear, and disempowerment that they experience. The state of their housing is critical indeed.

Our objective, then, is not to argue for the resolution of some temporary crisis and return to the status quo. We use the concept of crisis to highlight the ways that the contemporary housing system is unsustainable by its very nature. We point to the crisis tendencies in housing under contemporary capitalism, in order to draw attention to the urgent but systemic character of these problems.

In Defense of Housing

We do not seek to defend the housing system as it currently stands, which is in many ways indefensible. What needs defending is the use of housing as home, not as real estate. We are interested in the defense of housing as a resource that should be available to all.

Housing means many things to different groups. It is home for its residents and the site of social reproduction. It is the largest economic burden for many, and for others a source of wealth, status, profit, or control. It means work for those who construct, manage, and maintain it; speculative profit for those buying and selling it; and income for those financing it. It is a source of tax revenue and a subject of tax expenditures for the state, and a key component of the structure and functioning of cities.

Our concern is squarely with those who reside in and use housing—the people for whom home provides use values rather than exchange value. From the perspective of those who inhabit it, housing unlocks a whole range of social, cultural, and political goods. It is a universal necessity of life, in some ways an extension of the human body. Without it, participation in most of social, political, and economic life is impossible. Housing is more than shelter; it can provide personal safety and ontological security. While the domestic environment can be the site of oppression and injustice, it also has the potential to serve as a confirmation of one's agency, cultural identity, individuality, and creative powers.

The built form of housing has always been seen as a tangible, visual reflection of the organization of society. It reveals the existing class structure and power relationships. But it has also long been a vehicle for imagining alternative social orders. Every emancipatory movement must deal with the housing question in one form or another. This capacity to spur the political imagination is part of housing's social value as well.

Housing is the precondition both for work and for leisure. Controlling one's housing is a way to control one's labor as well as one's free time, which is why struggles over housing are always, in part, struggles over autonomy. More than any other item of consumption, housing structures the way that individuals interact with others, with communities, and with wider collectives. Where and how one lives decisively shapes the treatment one receives by the state and can facilitate relations with other citizens and with social movements. No other modern commodity is as important for organizing citizenship, work, identities, solidarities, and politics.

It is this side of housing—its lived, universally necessary, social dimension, and its identity as home—that needs defending. Our challenge as analysts, as residents, and as participants in housing struggles is to understand the causes and consequences of the multidimensional attack on housing. Our goal is to provide a critical understanding of the political-economic nature of housing, such that we may develop a greater sense of the actions needed to address housing's crises today and in the future.

1

Against the Commodification of Housing

On January 16, 2015, a limited liability corporation named P89-90 bought a single penthouse apartment in Midtown Manhattan for $100,471,452.77. The name of the actual buyer was kept secret, as were the identities of those who control the array of shell companies from around the world that own much of the rest of the building. It hardly matters, as the luxury tower that it tops, branded as One57, is not likely to be a particularly sociable environment. Chances are that none of the building's ninety-two condominium units will be their owner's sole residence. In fact, many of the apartments in One57 will remain empty. They will be held as investments or as vanity homes for people who do not lack for places to live. One57 is not high-rise housing so much as global wealth congealed into tower form.[1]

As One57 was constructed, across town in Bushwick, Brooklyn, residents of a vinyl-sided tenement building at 98

---

1   Vivian Marino, "$100.4 Million Sale at One57," *New York Times*, January 23, 2015; Andrew Rice, "Stash Pad," *New York Magazine*, June 29, 2014.

Linden Street saw their home being destroyed. Carlos Calero and five family members paid $706 per month for apartment 1L, a rent-stabilized two-bedroom apartment where they have lived for twenty years alongside friends and relatives. In 2012, the building was purchased in the name of Linden Ventures LLC. On the morning of June 4, 2013, the new owners allegedly hired a contractor to take a sledgehammer to the family's kitchen, bathroom, and floors. The apartment was left in ruins, and a campaign of harassment followed. According to New York City's Tenant Protection Unit, the landlords' purposeful destruction of their own building was part of an effort to drive out the Caleros and raise the rent, a strategy they have used in properties throughout the gentrifying Brooklyn neighborhoods of Bushwick, Williamsburg, and Greenpoint.[2]

In every corner of New York City, real estate is attacking housing. In some places it is evident in the weathering steel or blue glass that clads luxury towers. Elsewhere it can be seen in the shoddy materials used to subdivide apartments into tiny, fire-prone warrens. Sometimes the tactic is tenant harassment. Other times it is the state's power of eminent domain drafted

---

2   Kings County District Attorney, "Alleged Unscrupulous Landlords Indicted for Unlawful Eviction of Rent Stabilized Tenants and Filing False Documents in Connection with Residential Buildings in Bushwick, Greenpoint and Williamsburg," press release, April 16, 2015; Mireya Navarro, "2 Brooklyn Landlords, Accused of Making Units Unlivable, Are Charged with Fraud," *New York Times*, April 16, 2015; Chelsia Rose Marcius and Kenneth Lovett, "Landlord Accused of Trashing Apartments to Boot Rent-Regulated Tenants Hit with Subpoena by Gov. Cuomo," *New York Daily News*, April 24, 2014; Mireya Navarro, "Tenants Living amid Rubble in Rent-Regulated Apartment War," *New York Times*, February 24, 2014.

into the service of developers. These are all perverse manifestations of the same basic phenomenon: the subordination of the
social use of housing to its economic value.

What is happening in New York is happening around the
country and around the world. The form that the housing crisis
takes is different in Manhattan than in the foreclosed suburbs of
the American southwest, the bulldozed shacklands of South
Africa, the decanted council blocks of Great Britain, and the
demolished favelas of Brazil. But they have a common root:
they are all situations where the pursuit of profit in housing is
coming into conflict with its use for living.

Commodification is the name for the general process by
which the economic value of a thing comes to dominate its other
uses. Products "are only commodities because they have a dual
nature, because they are at the same time objects of utility and
bearers of value."[3] The commodification of housing means that
a structure's function as real estate takes precedence over its
usefulness as a place to live. When this happens, housing's role
as an investment outweighs all other claims upon it, whether
they are based upon right, need, tradition, legal precedent,
cultural habit, or the ethical and affective significance of the
home.[4]

---

3   Karl Marx, *Capital: A Critique of Political Economy*, vol. 1,
trans. Ben Fowkes (New York: Penguin, 1976 [1867]), 138.

4   On commodification and housing, see Peter Marcuse and
Emily Paradise Achtenberg, "Toward the Decommodification of
Housing," pp. 474–83 in Rachel G. Bratt, Chester Hartman, and
Ann Meyerson, eds, *Critical Perspectives on Housing* (Philadelphia:
Temple University Press, 1986), 477; Ray Forrest and Peter
Williams, "Commodification and Housing: Emerging Issues and
Contradictions," *Environment and Planning A* 16.9 (1984), 1163–80.

Our economic system is predicated on the idea that there is no conflict between the economic value-form of housing and its lived form. But across the world, we see those who exploit dwelling space for profit coming into conflict with those who seek to use housing as their home.

The Making of a Commodity

In the contemporary era it may be difficult to conceive of a housing system that is not ruled by the commodity form. Yet in the history of human settlements, the commodity treatment of dwelling space is relatively new.[5]

Historically, housing was not an independent sector of the economy. Rather, it was a by-product of broader social and economic relationships. When peasants were tied to the land, housing and work together formed the harsh feudal system to which they were yoked. Dwelling space was shaped by what Lewis Mumford describes as "the intimate union of domesticity and labor."[6] The loosening of this bond proceeded over centuries.

The historical precondition for the commodification of land and of housing was the privatization of the commons. Before land and housing could become exchangeable sources of privately appropriated profit, ancient systems of communal

---

5   This is obviously just an outline of a long and extremely complex historical process. For a more in-depth picture, see Arno Linklater, *Owning the Earth: The Transforming History of Landownership* (London: Bloomsbury Press, 2014); Lewis Mumford, *The City in History* (New York: Harcourt, 1989 [1961]).

6   Mumford, *The City in History*, 281.

regulation had to be swept away and traditional tenures destroyed. Marx calls this original or "primitive accumulation," when peasants are "suddenly and forcibly torn from their means of subsistence, and hurled onto the labour market as free, unprotected and rightless proletarians." This entire historical process is, Marx writes, "written in the annals of mankind in letters of blood and fire."[7]

The enclosure movement in early modern England was the classic example of primitive accumulation, and a crucial episode in the early development of capitalism.[8] In a sequence lasting centuries, common land was fenced off and claimed by individual landowners. Masses of dispossessed people migrated to cities, where they became laborers. For Karl Polanyi, this process constituted "a revolution of the rich against the poor," where the "lords and nobles . . . were literally robbing the poor of their share in the common, tearing down the houses which, by the hitherto unbreakable force of custom, the poor had long regard as theirs and their heirs'."[9]

Enclosure was a violent and complicated process that laid the groundwork for the eventual commodification of land on a planetary scale. What was accomplished in early modern

---

7 Marx, *Capital*, 875, 876.

8 On the enclosure movement, see J. M. Neeson, *Commoners: Common Rights, Enclosure and Social Change in England, 1700–1820* (Cambridge: Cambridge University Press, 1993); Barrington Moore, *The Social Origins of Democracy and Dictatorship: Lord and Peasant in the Making of the Modern World* (Boston: Beacon Press, 1966); Gilbert Slater, *The English Peasantry and the Enclosure of Common Fields* (New York: A. M. Kelley, 1968 [1907]).

9 Karl Polanyi, *The Great Transformation: The Political and Economic Origins of Our Time* (Boston, MA: Beacon Press, 2001 [1944]), 37.

Europe by the alliance of the landed aristocracy, large manufac-
turers, and "the new bankocracy"[10] was brought to the world
through colonialism. In the process, countless precolonial
systems of land tenure were destroyed.[11]

Even in early commercial-capitalist society, housing was
still predominantly shaped by the organization of work rather
than being produced as a commodity in its own right.[12] In
American colonial cities, households acted as integrated
economic units providing both the dwelling space and the
work space for the artisans, indentured servants, slaves, and
other laborers involved, willingly or not, in the value-
production process. "For artisans and merchants in the colonial city, the internal integration of house and shop, of living
space and work space, was social as well as spatial."[13] In
exchange for labor, property owners provided housing for

---

10   Marx, *Capital*, 885.

11   Which is not to say that privatization on a planetary scale
succeeded—only that various colonial projects tried to make it do so.
Even today there are ongoing struggles over enclosure wherever
property is held in common. See Stuart Hodkinson, "The New
Urban Enclosures," *CITY: Analysis of Urban Trends, Culture,
Theory, Policy, Action* 16.5 (2012), 500–18; Alex Vasudevan, Colin
McFarlane, and Alex Jeffrey, "Spaces of Enclosure," *Geoforum* 39
(2008), 1641–6; Nicholas Blomely, "Enclosure, Common Right and
the Property of the Poor," *Social and Legal Studies* 17.3 (2008),
311–31.

12   Cf. Peter Marcuse, "Gentrification, Homelessness, and the
Work Process: Housing Markets and Labour Markets in the
Quartered City," *Housing Studies* 4.3 (1989), 211–20.

13   Betsy Blackmar, "Re-walking the 'Walking City': Housing
and Property Relations in New York City, 1780–1840," *Radical
History Review* 21 (1979), 133.

their workers on terms ranging from violently exploitative to obligingly friendly.

Elsewhere, housing also remained stuck within traditional structures of landownership. In seventeenth-century England, for example, vast estates controlled by aristocratic families were usually held in trust, unable to be sold. A complex, speculative building-lease system developed in cities like London. Landlords maintained ownership of land that they leased for decades to builders, who might construct housing directly or sublease their plots to other builders. Rent gouging, displacement, and other features of the modern housing market emerged in what was in many ways still a feudal system.[14]

Even as industrialization and commercialism proceeded to transform urban space throughout Western societies, home and work remained connected—especially so for laborers. In the nineteenth-century metropolis, the sharp division between work and home was a sign of class privilege. Successful merchants and other wealthy urbanites created a world of domesticity that they sought to distinguish, architecturally and culturally, from the savage world of the market. Meanwhile, working-class households were forced to resort to homework, child labor, and taking in boarders.[15]

Slowly and fitfully, housing was disembedded from the circuits of work and production to become a direct bearer of

---

14   William C. Baer, "Is Speculative Building Underappreciated in Urban History?," *Urban History* 34.2 (2007), 302; Roy Porter, *London: A Social History* (Cambridge, MA: Harvard University Press, 1994), 103–4.

15   Ira Katznelson, *City Trenches: Urban Politics and the Patterning of Class in the United States* (Chicago: The University of Chicago Press, 1981), 38.

economic value in itself.[16] In the nineteenth century, Western cities came to feature an industrial proletariat no longer housed in—or chained to—their place of work. Now, for the first time, majorities of people looked to the open market to secure their place of residence. Cash payment became the main nexus between house and householder.[17] The conditions that enabled the commodification of housing had emerged.

In the 1840s, when Engels was surveying the dwelling conditions of the great towns of industrial Britain, he was in part describing the emerging impact of the commodification of housing.[18] The residential landscapes of industrial capitalism

---

16   Of course, as generations of feminist theorists have pointed out, for many the separation of work and home never happened. Especially at the height of the Fordist family wage system, women's unpaid domestic labor was central to the housing system. And other neo-feudal residential setups remain today, as in employer-owned housing. Our point here is not that the sphere of residence and the sphere of production were ever completely separated. It is that the market value of housing is no longer a function of the production that occurs within it.

17   Cf. "The bourgeoisie . . . has pitilessly torn asunder the motley feudal ties that bound man to his 'natural superiors', and has left remaining no other nexus between man and man than naked self-interest, than callous 'cash payment.'" Karl Marx and Friedrich Engels, *The Communist Manifesto*, trans. Samuel Moore (London: Penguin, 2002 [1848]), 220. The phrase "cash nexus" is a reference to the nostalgic conservative Thomas Carlyle—both conservatives and radicals alike developed separate critiques of the commodification of land. See Raymond Williams, *The Country and the City* (New York: Oxford University Press, 1973), 13–45.

18   Frederick [*sic*] Engels, *The Condition of the Working Class in England in 1844*, trans. Florence Kelley Wischnewetsky (London: Swan Sonnenschein, 1892 [1845]).

created enduring urban patterns. Industrialization saw the rise of new forms of segregation in metropolitan space and the unprecedented misery of the "slum problem" that, in Western cities, reached its peak in the late nineteenth and early twentieth centuries.[19] Even in this context, market forces did not operate alone. In cases where commodified housing did not provide adequate shelter to ensure the reproduction of the industrial workforce, some municipalities and charitable organizations built some of the earliest examples of social housing.

In the first decades of the twentieth century, it became clear that the commodification of dwelling space had proven to be a social disaster. Many governments moved to contain or neutralize the resulting unrest. Reformers created new rent regulations and building standards, and social housing was developed on a larger scale. At the same time, the value of housing within the overall political economy was becoming clearer. Residential and urban environments were becoming crucial circuits of investment that could act as an escape valve through which capital sought to manage the problem of over-accumulation.[20]

In the United States after World War I, Herbert Hoover, as secretary of commerce and later as president, promoted housing as the key to growing the consumer sector. By stoking demand for refrigerators, vacuum cleaners, washing machines, and other domestic appliances, the privately owned home became the

---

19   Peter Hall, *Cities of Tomorrow: An Intellectual History of Urban Planning and Design in the Twentieth Century*, 3rd ed. (Malden, MA: Blackwell, 2002 [1988]), 13–47.

20   See David Harvey, *The Limits to Capital* (Oxford: Blackwell, 1982).

heart, both economically and ideologically, of a world of commodities.[21]

When consumer purchasing power collapsed during the Great Depression, governments moved to shore up effective demand for housing. In response to the crisis posed by the Depression, the federal government created the regulatory structure that made the modern housing system possible. Through the Federal Housing Administration, the Glass-Steagall Act, and other New Deal initiatives, the standardized mortgage was born. Without this stabilizing federal presence, widespread homeownership would have been impossible. But in the process, government and real estate together used redlining, discrimination, and restrictive covenants to entrench racist patterns of land use and to exclude African-Americans from home finance, creating unjust housing patterns that continued to have destructive consequences far into the future.[22] The

---

21   Linklater, *Owning the Earth*, 349–50; Lawrence J. Vale, "The Ideological Origins of Affordable Homeownership Efforts," pp. 15–40 in William M. Rohe and Harry L. Watson, eds, *Chasing the American Dream: New Perspectives on Affordable Homeownership* (Ithaca, NY: Cornell University Press, 2007), 21–7.

22   Jesus Hernandez, "Redlining Revisited: Mortgage Lending Patterns in Sacramento 1930–2004," pp. 187–18 in Manuel Aalbers, ed., *Subprime Cities: The Political Economy of Mortgage Markets* (Malden, MA: Blackwell, 2012); Ira Katznelson, *When Affirmative Action Was White: The Untold History of Racial Inequality in Twentieth-Century America* (New York: Norton, 2006); Kevin Fox Gotham, "Racialization and the State: The Housing Act of 1934 and the Creation of the Federal Housing Administration," *Sociological Perspectives* 43.2 (2000), 291–317; Kenneth T. Jackson, *Crabgrass Frontier: The Suburbanization of the United States* (New York: Oxford University Press, 1985).

oppressive potential of the housing system, harking back to its function as a locus for the supply and exploitation of the work-force, was apparent—a function that was not in conflict with housing's commodity character, but supported by it.[23]

Many of the national housing systems that emerged after World War II had a partially decommodified character. In the socialist world, and in many countries throwing off the shack-les of colonialism, housing was established as a social right, and state-owned housing sectors accounted for most or all residential growth. In the growing Fordist–Keynesian econo-mies of the West, housing organized the mass consumption that underpinned mass production.[24] In the UK and other European countries, for example, national and local govern-ment built a majority of new homes.

In America's postwar boom years, the housing system was also anchored by state support. In some cases this involved the direct provision of dwelling space. But the postwar expansion of hous-ing in the United States did not take the form of the partial or total nationalization of the housing system that it did in Europe. Instead, it was built upon massive government investment in infrastructure and equally massive government action around mortgage lending to finance private dwellings with debt. The result was a state-supported system dominated by private owner-ship. Only in the 1940s did homeownership become the embodi-ment of the American dream. Throughout the first half of the

---

23 See chapter three, this volume.

24 See Michael Harloe, *The People's Home? Social Rented Housing in Europe and America* (Oxford: Blackwell, 1995); Richard L. Florida and Marshall M. A. Feldman, "Housing in U.S. Fordism," *International Journal of Urban and Regional Research* 12.2 (1988), 187–210.

twentieth century, less than half of Americans were homeowners. After 1950, ownership rates increased sharply. By 1980, more than 60 percent of Americans privately owned their homes.[25]

It was not until the second half of the twentieth century that housing would become a liquid asset and real estate a global, corporate behemoth. The commodity character of housing has ebbed and flowed. Its growth has been uneven and, as struggles worldwide demonstrate, it continues to be so. But it has always depended upon state action to make it possible. And it has never been a purely economic process—it has always had social and political dimensions.

The Age of Hyper-Commodification

If the extent of commodification expands and contracts historically, we are currently living through a period of unprecedented expansion. In today's transnational, digitally enhanced market, housing is becoming ever less an infrastructure for living and ever more an instrument for financial accumulation. The extreme ways in which housing is dominated by real estate today can be called hyper-commodification.

Under hyper-commodification, all of the material and legal structures of housing—buildings, land, labor, property rights— are turned into commodities. In the process, the capacity of a building to function as a home becomes secondary. What matters is how a building functions in circuits of economic accumulation.

---

25 William M. Rohe and Harry L. Watson, "Introduction: Homeownership in American Culture and Public Policy," pp. 1–12 in Rohe and Watson, *Chasing the American Dream*, 9.

The hyper-commodification of housing occurs in the context of broad political-economic developments that magnify its impact. Most significant is our era's growing inequality, which is reaching unprecedented levels. Inequality multiplies the power of economic elites, who benefit from the commodification of housing and then promote its further growth. Inequality also means that capital is on the offensive while the power of organized labor has been undercut. For working-class and poor people, wages have been stagnant for decades and, for many, consumption has been maintained through debt.[26] Lower wages for workers, paired with huge gains for the global elite, have meant many countries are more unequal now than they have been in over a century, or ever.[27]

This is also a time when housing and urbanization are becoming more central to the global economy. In many places, real estate has become more profitable and important than industry. Henri Lefebvre described this shift in 1970:

Real-estate speculation becomes the principal source for the formation of capital, that is, the realization of surplus value. As the percentage of overall surplus value formed and realized by industry begins to decline, the percentage created and realized by real-estate speculation and

---

26   Jon D. Wiseman, "Wage Stagnation, Rising Inequality and the Financial Crisis of 2008," *Cambridge Journal of Economics* 37.4 (2013), 921–45; William K. Tabb, "Wage Stagnation, Growing Insecurity, and the Future of the U.S. Working Class," *Monthly Review* 59.2 (2007), 20–30.

27   Organisation for Economic Co-operation and Development, *In It Together: Why Less Inequality Benefits All* (Paris: OECD Publishing, 2015).

construction increases . . . as economists are accustomed to saying, this is an unhealthy situation.[28]

Real estate and its allies in the finance and insurance sectors are no longer merely absorbing the shocks of the broader economy. They are increasingly calling the shots.

Beyond these broad trends, we can outline three more specific, interconnected, and mutually reinforcing factors that constitute the hyper-commodification of housing today. They are found in different varieties; some countries and cities have resisted one or another of them. But in one form or another, they are reshaping the housing systems of most of the countries and cities that participate in global neoliberal capitalism today.

The first factor is the contemporary counterpart to enclosure: *deregulation*, the removal of restrictions placed on real estate as a commodity. Throughout the United States and many other countries, there has been a steady trend towards weakening or abolishing the regulations, customs, and rules governing residential property.

The most obvious example is in home finance. Over the past few decades, regulations surrounding mortgage lending were fatally weakened in the United States, Britain, and many other countries. Pillars of financial regulation that constrained the mortgage market, like the Glass-Steagall Act, were gutted. Usury controls were eliminated. Competition was introduced into mortgage markets that had been tightly controlled. Variable interest rates, balloon payments, self-certification, interest-only loans, NINA ("no income, no assets") loans, and then

---

28   Henri Lefebvre, *The Urban Revolution*, trans. Robert Bononno (Minneapolis, MN: University of Minnesota Press, 2003 [1970]), 160.

eventually NINJA ("no income, no job, no assets") loans and other exotic mechanisms were introduced—and often sold to people who would have qualified for less expensive and less risky traditional mortgages. Predatory lending affected different communities unequally, and disproportionately destroyed the wealth of black and Latino households.[29] The regulatory powers that could have prevented these practices had been removed.[30]

Many other aspects of Western housing systems were deregulated as well. Rent regulation regimes have been overthrown.

29   This was, in part, made possible by the earlier exclusion of communities of color from major sources of housing finance. The racist impact of predatory finance is well established in the housing literature. See Hernandez, "Redlining Revisited"; Elvin Wyly and C. S. Ponder, "Gender, Age, and Race in Subprime America," *Housing Policy Debate* 21.4 (2011), 529–64; Gary A. Dymski, "Racial Exclusion and the Political Economy of the Subprime Crisis," *Historical Materialism* 17 (2009), 149–79; Elvin K. Wyly, Mona Atia, Holly Foxcroft, Daniel J. Hammel, and Kelly Phillips-Watts, "American Home: Predatory Mortgage Capital and Neighbourhood Spaces of Race and Class Exploitation in the United States," *Geografiska Annaler Series B Human Geography* 88.1 (2006), 105–32; Association of Community Organizations for Reform Now, "Separate and Unequal: Predatory Lending in America," 2004.

30   See Kevin Fox Gotham, "Creating Liquidity out of Spatial Fixity: The Secondary Circuit of Capital and the Restructuring of the US Housing Finance System," pp. 25–52 in Aalbers, *Subprime Cities*; Manuel B. Aalbers, "European Mortgage Markets before and after the Financial Crisis," pp. 120–50 in ibid.; Dan Immergluck, "Core of the Crisis: Deregulation, the Global Savings Glut, and Financial Innovation in the Subprime Debacle," *City and Community* 8.3 (2009), 341–5; Mark Stephens, "Mortgage Market Deregulation and Its Consequences," *Housing Studies* 22.2 (2007), 201–20.

Between 1981 and 2011, the number of rent-controlled apartments in New York plummeted from more than 285,000 to fewer than 39,000.[31] In the UK, the rental market underwent deregulation from the 1950s onward, accelerating in the 1980s and 1990s as part of a concerted effort to increase the number of private tenants.[32] The 1988 introduction of less secure tenancies created buy-to-let mortgages specifically for this purpose. Around a million such mortgages have been issued since then.[33]

Deregulation also permitted a wave of privatization of publicly owned or controlled housing. In the United States, public housing is in full retreat. Since the 1990s, more than 260,000 public housing units across the United States were either sold off to private owners or demolished in order to sell off the land beneath them.[34] The situation is even grimmer in Britain, where public housing represented a much larger piece of the residential sector. Since 1981, nearly 3 million units of council housing have been sold or

---

31   Furman Center for Real Estate and Urban Policy, *Rent Stabilization in New York City* (New York: New York University, 2012), 2.

32   Peter Malpass, "The Unraveling of Housing Policy in Britain," *Housing Studies* 11.3 (1996), 459–70; A. D. H. Cook, "Private Rented Housing and the Impact of Deregulation," pp. 91–112 in Johnston Birchall, ed., *Housing Policy in the 1990s* (New York: Routledge, 1992); Peter Malpass, *Reshaping Housing Policy: Subsidies, Rents and Residualisation* (London: Routledge, 1990).

33   John Bone and Karen O'Reilly, "No Place Called Home: The Causes and Social Consequences of the UK Housing 'Bubble,'" *British Journal of Sociology* 61.2 (2010), 238.

34   Center on Budget and Policy Priorities, "Introduction to Public Housing," January 25, 2013, 2; Edward G. Goetz, "Where Have All the Towers Gone? The Dismantling of Public Housing in U.S. Cities," *Journal of Urban Affairs* 33.3 (2011), 267–87.

transferred.[35] In the post-socialist world, the privatization of housing since 1989 has probably constituted the largest transfer of property rights in history.[36] The hard-won spaces of partial decommodification developed in the postwar period have been eroded.

For all of its far-reaching consequences, deregulation has not meant the subtraction of the state from real estate markets. It has not meant getting rid of regulations so much as rewriting them to make real estate a more liquid commodity. The state is still deeply involved throughout the housing system.

Second, and relatedly, housing has been undergoing a process of *financialization*. This is a generic term to describe the increasing power and prominence of actors and firms that engage in profit accumulation through the servicing and exchanging of money and financial instruments.[37] Managers, bankers, and *rentiers* produce profits from real estate through buying, selling, financing, owning, and

---

35   Norman Ginsburg, "The Privatisation of Council Housing," *Critical Social Policy* 25.1 (2005), 117. On the connection between public housing and gentrification in London, see Paul Watt, "Housing Stock Transfers, Regeneration and State-led Gentrification in London," *Urban Policy and Research* 27.3 (2009), 229–42.

36   Iván Tosics, "From Socialism to Capitalism: The Social Outcomes of the Restructuring of Cities," pp. 75–100 in Naomi Carmon and Susan S. Fainstein, eds, *Policy, Planning, and People: Promoting Justice in Urban Development* (Philadelphia, PA: University of Pennsylvania Press, 2013), 82.

37   See the literature on financialization: Costas Lapavitsas, "Financialised Capitalism: Crisis and Financial Expropriation," *Historical Materialism* 17 (2009), 114–48; John Bellamy Foster, "The Financialization of Capitalism," *Monthly Review* 58.11 (2007), 1–14; Greta R. Krippner, "The Financialization of the American Economy," *Socio-economic Review* 3.2 (2005), 173–208; Randy Martin, *Financialization of Daily Life* (Philadelphia: Temple University Press, 2002).

speculating. Players in this market often exchange in a disembodied, electronic realm. They need not ever see the actual physical buildings from which they make their fortunes—though their trading has serious consequence for those who occupy their properties.

Again, the mortgage market provides a good example. What was once a way to facilitate the production of housing has become a tool for profitmaking on its own. Over the past half-century or so, home mortgages were transformed from an industry dominated by local lending, thrifts, and passbook accounts to one dominated by global corporate banking and securitization. Government-sponsored enterprises like Fannie Mae and Freddie Mac have existed since the 1930s to supply liquidity to the mortgage market. But since the 1980s the practice of pooling mortgages and selling shares of their income stream has exploded.[38] Mortgage markets have become a way of turning solid structures into liquid assets. Houses can be bought and sold at the speed of electronic trade, and split into thousands of slices. As the housing scholar Desiree Fields puts it, "rather than anchoring wealth in place via property, today mortgages facilitate global investment and the extraction of value from place-bound property."[39] This was a process that financial firms enthusiastically promoted.

---

38   Kevin Fox Gotham, "The Secondary Circuit of Capital Reconsidered: Globalization and the U.S. Real Estate Sector," *American Journal of Sociology* 112.1 (2006), 257; Heather MacDonald, "The Rise of Mortgage-Backed Securities: Struggles to Reshape Access to Credit in the U.S.A.," *Environment and Planning A* 28.7 (1995), 1179.

39   Desiree Fields, "Contesting the Financialization of Urban Space: Community Organizations and the Struggle to Preserve Affordable Rental Housing in New York City," *Journal of Urban Affairs* 37.2 (2014), 148. See also Gotham, "Creating Liquidity Out of Spatial Fixity"; Manuel B. Aalbers, "The Financialization of Home and the Mortgage Market Crisis," *Competition and Change* 12.2 (2008), 148–66.

Under financialization, the nature of the real estate company is changing. Traditionally, real estate even in big cities was a local and relatively small-scale affair. Merchants, professionals, and others with capital to invest would leverage their money and social networks as landlords.[40] Even in cities like New York, real estate has been ruled by thousands of small players led by a few powerful family firms.

But the real estate ecosystem is being colonized by large-scale corporate finance. Wall Street and the City of London are the new landlords on the block. Private equity is becoming a major presence in the housing markets of New York and other cities, expanding its role greatly since the mid-2000s. Between 2004 and 2008, private-equity firms went on a buying binge, cumulatively purchasing 90,000 rent-stabilized apartments in New York City, nearly 10 percent of the total number of units.[41] Throughout America, companies like JP Morgan Chase, Blackstone, and Colony Capital have been buying up single-family homes in suburban and exurban areas hard hit by foreclosure since 2007. Industry analysts see cornering this market as their "$1.5 trillion opportunity."[42]

---

40   Michael Harloe, "The Recommodification of Housing," pp. 17–50 in Michael Harloe and Elizabeth Lebas, eds, *City, Class and Capital: New Developments in the Political Economy of Cities and Regions* (London: Edward Arnold, 1981), 26.

41   Association for Neighborhood and Housing Development, "The Sub-prime Loan Crisis in New York Apartment Housing: How Collapsing Predatory Equity Deals Will Harm Communities and Investors in New York City" (2008), 3.

42   The Homes for All Campaign of the Right to the City Alliance, principal author Desiree Fields, "The Rise of the Corporate Landlord: The Institutionalization of the Single-Family Rental Market and Potential Impacts on Renters" (2014), 6.

The growth of real estate investment trusts (REITs) is one measure of the financialization of housing. In the United States, REITs were created by Congressional law in 1960. They spent their early years as mere tax shelters. But another act of Congress in 1986 gave them the ability to take a more active role in operating and exploiting the buildings in their portfolios. Since then their numbers and their reach have grown exponentially. REITs comprise the largest property owners in New York, including firms like Vornado and SL Green.

Finally, commodification is reinforced by the *globalization* of housing. Residential real estate may be fixed in place, but it is increasingly dominated by economic networks that are global in scope. Daniel Rose, a New York real estate insider, told an industry conference in 2002,

> Only a few years ago, New York structures were built, financed, owned, managed and occupied by New Yorkers, just as those in Chicago or London, San Francisco or Paris were controlled locally. In today's globalized world, capital, ideas, and people flow freely across state and national borders . . . Many of the people in this very room have no idea that the net cash flow from the apartment or office rent they pay in New York finds its way to investors in Germany or in England.[43]

Real estate has become a worldwide colossus. Starting in the late 1990s, direct investment abroad by US real estate companies increased sharply.[44] Foreign direct investment in US real estate

---

43 Daniel Rose, "Real Estate: Evolution of an Industry," *Real Estate Issues* 28.3 (2003), 49.

44 Gotham, "The Secondary Circuit of Capital Reconsidered," 247.

has also grown, increasing from $2 billion in 1973 to more than $50 billion in 2002.[45]

The involvement of foreigners in housing is not a problem on its own. But the ways in which housing is undergoing globalization are symptomatic of the decoupling of housing from residential needs. Some housing markets are starting to become more responsive to global economic signals than to local ones. In London, New York, and elsewhere, units in new apartment buildings are regularly advertised to foreign buyers, sometimes before being offered to locals. Governments sell their housing stock to international investors at property fairs such as Le marché international des professionnels de l'immobilier, known as MIPIM.[46] In these cases, housing is directly connected to global circuits as an investment. At that distance, its use as living space barely registers.

Dwelling in the Commodity Form

Together, these interlocking processes of deregulation, financialization, and globalization have meant that housing functions as a commodity to a greater extent than ever before. This is what lies at the heart of the present crisis.

What does it mean to dwell in a hyper-commodified world? The consequences of the transformation of housing can be

---

45   Ibid., 246. These figures are in constant 2002 dollars.

46   Oliver Wainwright, "Anger at Cannes Property Fair Where Councils Rub Shoulders with Oligarchs," *The Guardian*, March 14, 2014; Martina Fuchs and André Scharmanski, "Counteracting Path Dependencies: 'Rational' Investment Decisions in the Globalising Commercial Property Market," *Environment and Planning A* 41.11 (2009), 2724–40.

felt throughout the housing system, but they are extremely uneven.

In the most expensive districts of the world, luxury buildings proliferate out of all proportion to actual housing need. The super-rich own huge amounts of real estate, much of which is used purely for investment. The head of a New York real estate brokerage gleefully described "luxury real estate as the world's new currency."[47] Exclusive addresses in cities like London, New York, Tokyo, Miami, Paris, Shanghai, Moscow, Hong Kong, and Vancouver have become favorable places to park a fortune. "The global elite," the developer Michael Stern remarked to a reporter, "is basically looking for a safe-deposit box."[48]

So-called super-prime real estate is cloaked in secrecy. Cash-only purchases and layer upon layer of holding companies can disguise dubious fortunes. Numerous observers have tied the rise of luxury housing to money laundering, tax evasion, and other illegal transactions.[49] Property owners in prestige locations—Ostozhenka in Moscow; the blocks surrounding Central Park in Manhattan; the Bishops Avenue in Hampstead,

---

47   Jonathan Miller, "Luxury Real Estate as the World's New Currency," *Douglas Elliman Magazine*, October 18, 2012, 16.

48   Rice, "Stash Pad."

49   Damien Gayle, "Foreign Criminals Use London Housing Market to Launder Billions of Pounds," *The Guardian*, July 25, 2015; Martin Filler, "New York: Conspicuous Construction," *New York Review of Books*, April 2, 2015; Michael Hudson, Ionuț Stanescu, and Sam Adler-Bell, "How New York Real Estate Became a Dumping Ground for the World's Dirty Money," *The Nation*, July 3, 2014; Hans Nelen, "Real Estate and Serious Forms of Crime," *International Journal of Social Economics* 35.10 (2008), 751–62.

London—have been linked to criminal activity.[50] The "starchitect" designs and posh addresses seem calculated to hide the fact that, according to one sociologist, in some of these landed exclaves of the offshore world, forms of corporate, personal, and criminal capital are becoming "progressively undifferentiated."[51]

Plenty of super-prime real estate should barely be considered housing at all. Many luxury buildings are not built primarily to provide housing but to make profits upon resale. The value of super-prime real estate is secure because of the ease with which it can be converted into money through loans, debentures, mortgages, and other complex financial transactions. Whether anyone will ever make a home in such buildings is irrelevant. New York City's Independent Budget Office estimates that only about half of the units in expensive newer buildings are primary residences,[52] and the true figure may be far lower. The few people who do reside in many newer high-end buildings report neighborless empty hallways.[53] In London, areas with heavy concentrations of super-prime housing lack

---

50   Robert Booth, "UK Properties Held by Offshore Firms Used in Global Corruption, Say Police," *The Guardian*, March 4, 2015; Louise Story and Stephanie Saul, "Stream of Foreign Wealth Flows to Elite New York Real Estate," *New York Times*, February 7, 2015; Sophia Kishkovsky, "A Class Struggle on Moscow's Golden Mile," *International Herald Tribune*, December 18, 2006.

51   John Urry, *Offshoring* (Cambridge: Polity, 2014), 20; William Brittain-Catlin, *Offshore: The Dark Side of the Global Economy* (New York: Farrar, Straus, and Giroux, 2005).

52   New York City Independent Budget Office, "Budget Options for New York City," November 2014, 50.

53   Elizabeth A. Harris, "Why Buy a Condo You Seldom Use? Because You Can," *New York Times*, February 11, 2013.

foot traffic or other signs of life. Local businesses can have trouble staying open.[54]

In brief, luxury housing is antisocial. The people who own these properties may have no connection to the places where they park their money. Lefebvre had already recognized this dynamic in the 1960s: "the Olympians of the new bourgeois aristocracy no longer inhabit. They go from grand hotel to grand hotel, or from castle to castle, commanding a fleet or a country from a yacht. They are everywhere and nowhere."[55] Research has demonstrated that the super-wealthy use their resources to avoid encounters with poverty, conflict, difference, and other elements of what they see as the downside of urban life.[56]

The trickle-down benefits of such high-priced housing have been greatly exaggerated. Due to the vagaries of local development policies, owners of these buildings frequently pay little or no tax, and many enjoy huge public subsidies. One57 received more than $65 million in public subsidies and tax breaks.[57] The idea with such subsidies is that developers of luxury buildings

---

54   For an analysis of how elites are transforming one part of London, see Richard Webber and Roger Burrows, "Life in an Alpha Territory: Discontinuity and Conflict in an Elite London 'Village,'" forthcoming in *Urban Studies*.

55   Henri Lefebvre, "The Right to the City," pp. 63–181 in Eleonore Kofman and Elizabeth Lebas, eds and trans., *Writings on Cities* (Oxford: Blackwell, 1996 [1967]), 158–9.

56   Rowland Atkinson, "Limited Exposure: Social Concealment, Mobility and Engagement with Public Space by the Super-Rich in London," *Environment and Planning A* (forthcoming), 1–16.

57   See New York City Independent Budget Office, "From Tax Breaks to Affordable Housing: Examining the 421-a Tax Exemption for One57," July 2015.

can be incentivized to construct less-exclusive units as well. But among other problems, this system produces glaring inefficiencies.[58] New York's recently rebranded Billionaire's Row, the stretch of ultra-expensive condominiums on West 57th Street, has so far contributed a grand total of eighty-nine affordable apartments to the city.[59] One57's developers contributed sixty-six homes at a cost of $905,000 per unit. The Independent Budget Office calculated that a grant of that size in the hands of a nonprofit housing organization could have built 370 apartments at a cost of only $179,000 per unit.[60] More homes owned by billionaires contribute little to the communities in which they stand. But they still take up space, force up costs, and push others farther out.

While it facilitates the over-accumulation of luxury for the wealthy, the hyper-commodification of housing leads to new forms of risk, unaffordability, and instability for everyone else.

The current phase of housing commodification has not translated into the affordable paradise that its promoters predicted. Instead, it has allowed powerful elites to monopolize more housing. Cities like New York that have seen extensive deregulation and huge building booms in recent decades have not seen corresponding drops in housing costs. One international study found that "demand pressures stemming from financial

---

58   The major issue is that "affordable housing" is a real estate strategy, not a mechanism for producing decent housing that everyone can afford. See chapter four, this volume.

59   Rosa Goldensohn, "Billionaire's Row Supertower Deal Only Subsidized About 23 Affordable Units," DNAinfo.com, July 30, 2015.

60   New York City Independent Budget Office, "Tax Breaks to Affordable Housing."

deregulation may have translated into increases in house prices by some 30 percent."[61] Globalized, deregulated markets are unstable and subject to wild price swings, first contributing to bubbles and later to crashes.[62]

Increasingly, there are no alternatives to commodified housing. Public housing and rent regulation, the spaces of partial decommodification in New York, are disappearing. Between 1981 and 2011, the regulated share of the rental market fell from more than 62 percent to 47 percent of all units.[63] As a result, the rental market is more precarious for tenants. Between 2001 and 2014, real rents in the United States rose by 7 percent, while in the same period real household income fell by 9 percent.[64] More households are forced to compete with one another in a less regulated market controlled by bigger corporate firms. Many of the new landlords entering the rental market have not shown enthusiasm for improving the situation for their tenants. Renters

---

61   Dan Andrews, Aida Caldera Sánchez, and Åsa Johansson, "Housing Markets and Structural Policies in OECD Countries," *OECD Economics Department Working Papers* 836 (2011), 7; Nick Bailey, "Deregulated Private Renting: A Decade of Change in Scotland," *Netherlands Journal of Housing and the Built Environment* 14.4 (1999), 363–84. See also David G. Green and Daniel Bentley, "Finding Shelter: Overseas Investment in the UK Housing Market" (London: Civitas, 2014).

62   Michael McCord, Stanley McGreal, Jim Berry, Martin Haran, and Peadar Davis, "The Implications of Mortgage Finance on Housing Market Affordability," *International Journal of Housing Markets and Analysis* 4.4 (2011), 394–417.

63   Furman Center, *Rent Stabilization in New York City*.

64   Joint Center for Housing Studies, "America's Rental Housing: Expanding Options for Diverse and Growing Demand" (2015), 4.

of REIT-owned houses in California report paying higher-than-average rents and shouldering the burden of home repairs on their own.[65]

In the United Kingdom, tenants are also facing a new world of exploitation and insecurity. Public housing is being disman-tled, and, as a result, tenants must turn to private landlords—sometimes the same people who cannibalized the public hous-ing stock in the first place. In one development in South London, more than forty ex-public-housing units are owned by the son of the government minister who presided over the privatization of public housing in the 1980s.[66] In London as whole, more than 36 percent of former publicly owned units are now rented out privately; in some local areas this figure is more than 50 percent.[67]

In a notable example of housing policy absurdity, some UK tenants in ex-public-housing units receive public subsidy for their rent, which they pay to private landlords.[68] One tenant on a council estate told reporters that she is charged £800 per month

---

65   Aimee Inglis, principal author, "The New Single-Family Home Renters of California: A Statewide Survey of Tenants Renting from Wall Street Landlords" (Tenants Together, May 2015); Rob Call, principal author, "Renting from Wall Street: Blackstone's Invitation Homes in Los Angeles and Riverside" (Right to the City Alliance, 2014).

66   Nick Sommerland, "Great Tory Housing Shame: Third of Ex-Council Homes Now Owned by Rich Landlords," *Daily Mirror*, March 5, 2013; David Spittles, "Ex-Council Flats Are Right to a Goldmine," *Homes and Property*, July 25, 2012.

67   Tom Copley, *From Right to Buy to Buy to Let* (London: Greater London Authority/London Assembly Labour, January 2014), 2.

68   Ibid.

by a private landlord, while her council rent for the same unit would have been £360 per month—with the public making up the shortfall.[69] The whole situation typifies hyper-commodified housing: profit-seeking businesses inserting themselves into the residential system and siphoning off resources, making housing more expensive while contributing nothing to the ability of the system to meet residents' needs.

Commodification and Gentrification

For the corporate investors buying up housing throughout New York, gentrification is the business plan. Firms purchase buildings on the assumption that rents can be doubled, tripled, or more. This strategy is predicated upon taking units out of the rent stabilization system—in effect, recommodifying housing—and displacing lower-income tenants.[70]

Take the case of Zhi Qin Zheng, a founding member of New York's Chinatown Tenants Union and a former garment worker in her sixties. When an investment company named Madison Capital bought the downtown Manhattan building where she lived in a rent-stabilized unit, it determined that what she saw as her longtime, affordable home was in fact an "underperforming asset." Her home needed to be "repositioned" to garner the sixfold rent increase that the market supposedly demanded in the name of efficiency. So her landlord, according to reports, began a campaign of

---

69   Nick Sommerland, "Ex-Council Housing Racket: Private Landlords Charging Several Times Council Levels with Taxpayer Footing Difference," *Daily Mirror*, March 6, 2013.

70   See Harloe, "The Recommodification of Housing."

harassment—cutting the heat, leaving damage unrepaired, and gratuitously calling the police on tenants in a campaign that residents saw as "aimed at pushing them and their culture out of the buildings."[71]

Landlord associations say that only the few proverbial bad apples break the law. But this basic story—a building that is seen to be underperforming is reorganized to generate more income—happens every day across the city. It is a pure form of what the geographer Neil Smith saw as the essence of gentrification: claiming the gap between the current rent and a building's "highest and best use."[72] When housing units are bought on the assumption that they can be turned into more liquid commodities, displacement is the predictable result.

Low-income tenants who cannot afford higher rents maintain a foothold in gentrifying neighborhoods in two ways. Either they are protected by some form of partial decommodification, such as rent control or public housing—policies which, as we have shown, are being actively undermined by the day—or they are lucky enough to have an economically irrational landlord. This is a risky prospect in a competitive real estate

---

71   Elizabeth Dwoskin, "When Hipsters Move in on Chinese: It's Ugly," *Village Voice*, April 20, 2010; Michael Powell, "Her Chinatown Home Is 'Underperforming,'" *New York Times*, August 15, 2011; Lore Croghan, "Chinatown Divided: Luxury Developers Battle Tenants and Small-Business Owners," *New York Daily News*, March 5, 2009. See CAAAV Organizing Asian Communities and the Community Development Project of the Urban Justice Center, *Converting Chinatown: A Snapshot of a Neighborhood Becoming Unaffordable and Unlivable* (New York: CAAV, December 2008).

72   Neil Smith, *The New Urban Frontier: Gentrification and the Revanchist City* (New York: Routledge, 1996), 62.

environment, but it does allow some tenants a modicum of stability. A New York community organizer told housing researchers,

> Landlords are not always maximising their income. Many things affect the decisions of landlords. There are members of the community, there are thousands and thousands of disabled people and older people, for example, who pay far below the market rate and have been for a long time because the landlord knows them and has a relationship with them. He makes this illogical decision and that's why the old lady comes in and has been paying $600 for the last decade. There are community values that mediate the market. Not 100 per cent but in many cases, there is a community consensus that we shouldn't evict the disabled, single person; this mediates the pressure to raise the rents.[73]

The onward march of commodification makes situations like this unlikely. The community organizer continued, "As the market rate goes up and up, that consensus breaks down."[74] Shareholders may live scattered across the world and only own a share in a property on a short-term basis. They have no patience for such irrational behavior. The economic and organizational logic demands that rents be raised as high as possible.

This is not to say that this strategy always turns a profit.

---

73   Kathe Newman and Elvin K. Wyly, "The Right to Stay Put, Revisited: Gentrification and Resistance to Displacement in New York City," *Urban Studies* 43.1 (2006), 49.

74   Ibid.

Buildings can easily fail to generate the desired returns. But even when this happens, there is no exit from the commodified housing system—and no clear mechanism whereby failed real estate projects might be reappropriated by residents as common property. Foreclosed buildings are just reinserted into financialized circuits, setting up a repeat of the entire process. Rent-regulated buildings in the Bronx purchased by Ocelot Capital in 2007, for example, fell into foreclosure and in the following years cycled through a series of owners, falling into an ever-worsening state of repair.[75]

Commodification is a self-reproducing process. And it operates simultaneously at different scales: at the scale of the neighborhood, the building, and even the household. Hence the practice of subletting spare rooms or sofas—the commodification of ever-smaller spaces becomes a strategy for eking out a place in an unstable and expensive housing market. This too gets absorbed into a broader instrumental logic. One self-styled "rent-to-rent" entrepreneur in London explained straightforwardly to a reporter, "I rent a property with a view to renting it out at a higher rent."[76] No doubt some canny financial innovators are already working on the securitization of rent-to-rent housing or the pooling of income streams from subletting.

---

75 Dina Levy, "Fighting Predatory Equity," *Shelterforce*, March 29, 2011.

76 Patrick Collinson, "Meet the New Class of Landlords Profiting from Generation Rent," *The Guardian*, June 28, 2013; Emma Lunn and Patrick Collinson, "Rent-to-Rent, the Latest Get-Rich-Quick Scheme," *The Guardian*, June 29, 2013.

Unleashing the Cranes

Some observers argue that the unprecedented shift towards the commodification of housing has not gone far enough. There are many voices today that declare that if real estate developers were just given a freer hand, then the market would solve the housing crisis.

For example, the economist Edward Glaeser argues, "The best way to make cities more affordable is to reduce the barriers to building and unleash the cranes. To do so, end the dizzying array of land use regulations in most cities that increase cost."[77] The conservative housing scholar Howard Husock contends that New York must "thaw its frozen housing market" by getting rid of rent stabilization and public housing.[78] The liberal writer Matthew Yglesias also affirms a "deregulatory agenda."[79] For these authors and more, the hyper-commodification of housing is not the problem—it is the solution.

This reasoning follows clearly from standard economic logic. But this position ignores the real-world effects of the commodification of housing. Fully deregulating and unleashing the cranes will not and cannot solve the housing crisis, for a number of reasons.

First, while markets are imagined as self-organizing entities, as we have seen, the state has always been central to the process of making housing a commodity that can circulate through market exchange. The state cannot "get out" of housing markets

---

77   Edward Glaeser, "Ease Housing Regulation to Increase Supply," *New York Times*, October 16, 2013.

78   Howard Husock, "The Frozen City," *City Journal* (2013).

79   Matthew Yglesias, "NIMBYS Are Killing the National Economy," *Vox*, April 25, 2014.

because the state is one of the institutions that creates them. Government sets the rules of the game. It enforces the sanctity of contracts, establishes and defends regimes of property rights, and plays a central role in connecting the financial system to the bricks and mortar in which people dwell.

In other words, housing markets are political all the way down. The balance of power between tenants and landlords, or between real estate owners and communities, cannot be determined in a neutral, apolitical way. What the free market boosters ignore is the question of power.

The housing market is, among other things, a domain of struggle between different, unequal groups. Removing the regulations that rein in property owners shifts power towards capital and away from residents—while also, not coincidentally, making land more valuable and more amenable to speculation. This is why it is the real estate lobby that campaigns to deregulate the housing system, a demand that tenants almost never make. The commodification of housing is a political project that refuses to acknowledge itself as such.

Supporters of deregulation argue that zoning, rent control, and tenant protections are only pursued by meddling bureaucrats or greedy residents. But the real estate industry does whatever it can to maintain high prices. Removing existing tenant protections would just place real estate firms in a better position to reshape markets even more in their own favor.

Second, when housing becomes a globalized, financialized commodity, the gulf widens between the price signals to which markets respond and the actual social need for dwelling space.

Investment firms chasing short-term gains reorient the housing system away from local residential needs and disconnect prices from wages in local labor markets. Transnational speculation begins to shape what gets built, where it appears, and who can afford to live in it. We see this happening in cities like London and Vancouver, home to increasing numbers of apartments that are ill-suited to the families who need to live in them but easily sold to investors who live abroad.

There is a world of difference between economic demand and social need. Many people, especially poor and working-class households, need more housing than they can afford. But this form of need does not register with purely profit-oriented developers. Far from responding efficiently to residential needs, investors can turn a profit by squeezing more money out of existing spaces while adding nothing to the general housing stock. Developers routinely engage in land hoarding and other strategies centered on speculation and scarcity.

Even some economists recognize that housing markets are structurally incapable of being efficient.[80] It is easy to inflate price bubbles and difficult to deflate them. The history of real estate is replete with speculation.[81] Despite how it appears in abstract models, the actual market in housing is neither efficient nor rational.

Those who want to unleash the cranes will counter that "distortions" in housing markets must be due to government regulation rather than to market dynamics as such. Displacement

---

80   For an incisive discussion of the role of the efficient-market hypothesis in the subprime crisis see Gary A. Dymski, "The Reinvention of Banking and the Subprime Crisis: On the Origins of Subprime Loans, and How Economists Missed the Crisis," pp. 151–84 in Aalbers, *Subprime Cities*.

81   Robert J. Shiller, "The Housing Market Still Isn't Rational," *New York Times*, July 24, 2015; Edward L. Glaeser, "A Nation of Gamblers: Real Estate Speculation and American History," National Bureau of Economic Research Working Paper, 2013.

would not be a problem, they say, had there not been rent regulation in the first place. State interference creates distortions, they argue, so deregulation is necessary in the name of removing inefficiencies.

But we need to question this definition of efficiency. One person's inefficiency is another person's home. We need to ask why investors' profits should trump the needs of residents. From the perspective of a tenant facing displacement from their longtime home, it is the system of commodified residential development that is inefficient, not to mention cruel and destructive. That a building has become a target for speculators due to changes in global housing markets in no way lessens its usefulness as living space for its inhabitants.

Supporters of deregulation offer the process of filtering as a *deus ex machina* that will provide affordable housing. But in practice, there are limits to the stock of old buildings, especially within specific neighborhoods. And filtering today often takes the form of older buildings being recouped by wealthier households.

This touches on the final reason why markets will not solve the housing crisis. Those who want to deregulate and build do not consider the practical consequences of commodification in action.

It may be true that, all other things remaining equal, enlarging supply while keeping demand constant would lead to lower prices. But stated that way, the claim is too abstract. All other things would not remain equal. Promoters of free-market housing solutions never consider the costs and consequences that would result from attempting to establish a purely self-regulating market in housing.

Setting up the conditions for frictionless exchange and unlimited development could in theory create a situation

where the price of housing falls until it is affordable to everyone including the lowest paid workers. But trying to reach that
point would entail overturning the existing residential landscape. It would mean displacement on an immense scale. It
would make it easier for landlords to threaten, harass, and
exploit tenants. It would lead to huge increases in residential
segregation. It would encourage shoddy, dangerous conversions and environmental degradation. It would lead to the
proliferation of under-maintained, overcrowded, dangerous
dwellings; such buildings were pervasive during the heyday of
laissez-faire housing in the late nineteenth century. The idea
that tenants in a fully unregulated market could avoid such
harmful conditions just by exercising consumer choice is
naïve. And it is unrealistic to imagine that there would not be
some countermovement in response.

Towards Decommodification

Around the world, those seeking to turn houses into liquid assets
are creating problems for those who merely want to live in them.
And yet the ideological glorification of the free market is stronger
than ever. It is becoming harder to visualize any alternatives other
than minor modifications in the pattern here or there—or even to
see the commodified housing system for what it is.

Commodification is not the default state that housing adopts. It
is relatively new. It depends upon state action. It differs according
to time and place and mutates in response to changing conditions.
And its consequences are uneven, helping the super-wealthy
generate huge profits while creating instability for the rest.

In *The Great Transformation*, Karl Polanyi demonstrated that
"the idea of a self-adjusting market implied a stark utopia. Such

an institution could not exist for any length of time without annihilating the human and natural substance of society."[82] The idea of a self-adjusting housing market is similarly utopian.

In unequal contexts where the logic of commodification rules, some people will always be forced into uninhabitable dwelling spaces. Some will live in sheds, some in closets. Some will live amid toxic pollution. Some will be packed with twenty-five other people, including children, into a single home.[83] These are not market failures—they are how the market works.

Ultimately, the problem with making housing a commodity is that as such, living space will be distributed based on the ability to pay and provided to the extent that it produces a profit. But ability to pay is unequal while the need for a place to live is universal. There is thus an unavoidable contradiction.

No matter how many actors and institutions treat it as such, housing can never be a fully liquid, exchangeable commodity. Its use value, and indeed a portion of its monetary value, comes from its place within communities that emerge over time. They require continuity and stability. Wrenching housing out of its context obliterates this social dimension.

In the end, however, we cannot blame real estate companies for today's housing injustices. As entities created, using the

---

82   Polanyi, *The Great Transformation*, 3.

83   These are all recent examples from various cities. See Amelia Gentleman, "The Woman Who Lives in a Shed: How London Landlords Are Cashing in," *The Guardian*, May 9, 2012; "In Wealthy Hong Kong, Poorest Live in Metal Cages," *New York Daily News*, August 2, 2013; Make the Road New York, *Toxic Homes: Exposure to Indoor Toxins in Bushwick* (New York: Make the Road, 2009); Patrick Butler, "Housing Raid Finds 26 People Living in Three-Bedroom East London Home," *The Guardian*, June 25, 2015.

legal powers of the state, for the sole purpose of economic accumulation, corporations are single-minded by design. Profit seeking without regard for external social consequences is intrinsic to the way they are set up. Residential inequality and crisis will always result from a housing system dominated by these kinds of firms and by other property owners following the same logic.

The solution to the housing problem, then, is not moralism, but the creation of an alternative residential logic. Exhorting for-profit real estate companies to act differently in the name of creating a less vicious housing system is pointless. Housing problems are not the result of greed or dishonesty. They result from the structural logic of the current housing system. Alternative, decommodified models of residential development must therefore be created. Far from stopping new construction, cities need more new decommodified dwellings, such as public or cooperative housing. A proper understanding of the housing crisis today requires an account of its commodification. Making real progress on housing problems requires developing concrete alternatives to it.

2

Residential Alienation

In 2012, Mahamadou and Assetu Tounkara and their six children were living together in one small room in the South Bronx. The Tounkaras' overcrowded space was part of a three-bedroom apartment that also housed two other families. The Tounkaras were on a waiting list for a spot in New York City public housing. They had already been waiting for four years. Given that the list included 160,000 other families, their chances of landing a unit were slim.

Mahamadou, an auto mechanic who moved to the Bronx from Mali in 1996, was not optimistic about their residential prospects. "It's hard to live like this," he told a reporter. "You want more space, but if you don't have money, how are you going to pay for it?" With a family income of $1,700 per month, decent, affordable, and secure housing in New York is nearly impossible to find.[1]

---

1 Winnie Hu, "Some See Little Room for Large, Poor Families in Mayor's Housing Plan," *New York Times*, October 19, 2012.

On a low income in an expensive city that offers them few housing alternatives, the Tounkara family, with eight people in one room, face particularly difficult challenges. But their situation is all too common. The South Bronx is not a dependable source of affordable housing—rents are rising rapidly as corporate investors set their sights on the borough. And across New York City, an estimated 12 percent of all rental units are overcrowded.[2] Twenty other families that Mahamadou and Assetu knew from their local mosque put up with similarly cramped conditions.

Living this way is not only uncomfortable. It can have deadly consequences. Overcrowding was a factor in the 2007 fire that broke out in a building on Woodycrest Avenue in the Bronx, killing eight children and one adult, also Malian immigrants.[3]

The political and economic elites who make the decisions that shape the housing system tend to experience their dwellings as secure havens. They use their homes as tools for personal fulfillment, economic accumulation, and social advancement.

But this is far from reality for many households. Growing numbers of people today do not feel at home in their housing. Overcrowding, displacement, dispossession, homelessness, harassment, disrepair, and other ordeals are increasingly common. Adequate, stable, affordable dwelling space is becoming ever more scarce. As a result, many people experience their housing as just another precarious place in an insecure world.

---

2   New York City Rent Guidelines Board, *Housing Supply Report* (New York: New York City Rent Guidelines Board, 2015), 3.

3   Michael Wilson, "8 Children Are Among Dead in Bronx Fire," *New York Times*, March 8, 2007.

There is a term for not feeling at home that has a long history in social science and critical theory: *alienation*.[4] The idea of "feeling at home" seems to be the very opposite of alienation. Applying the notion of alienation to the residential sphere can help us understand the experience of residential struggles today—and illuminate the connections between housing crisis and personal crisis.

The extent and nature of residential alienation vary dramatically between different groups and different places. Some countries and cities offer more security than others. But residential alienation can be found across the world. It is the product of the hyper-commodification of housing, the casualization of employment, rising inequality, and the neoliberal assault on the social safety net. These processes affect owner-occupiers as well as tenants, and middle-class households as well as working-class ones. Their impact is felt unevenly, but it is a mistake to suppose that they are only a problem for the poorest households.

In a time when flexibility is affirmed above stability, and when many major institutions designed to shield people from risk are undergoing their own crises, the growth of precarity and

---

4   We obviously only scratch the surface of this concept here. For in-depth analyses of alienation, see Sean Sayers, *Marx and Alienation: Essays on Hegelian Themes* (Basingstoke: Palgrave Macmillan, 2011); Lauren Langman and Devorah Kalekin-Fishman, *The Evolution of Alienation: Trauma, Promise and the Millennium* (Oxford: Rowman & Littlefield, 2006); Bertell Ollman, *Alienation: Marx's Concept of Man in Capitalist Society*, 2nd ed. (Cambridge: University of Cambridge Press, 1976); Richard Schact, *Alienation* (New York: Doubleday, 1970); Istán Mészáros, *Marx's Theory of Alienation* (London: Merlin Press, 1970); Erich Fromm, *Marx's Concept of Man* (New York: F. Ungar, 1961).

alienation should not be surprising.[5] But the impact of this process on the experience of dwelling does not penetrate mainstream housing politics. If we want to truly understand the consequences of the hyper-commodification of housing, we need to understand the alienated psychosocial experience—the fear, stress, anxiety, and disempowerment—that the current housing system produces.

Alienation and Housing

Alienation means estrangement, objectification, or othering. The idea is rarely applied to housing, but it should be. Intuitively, alienation belongs within the field of housing, almost uniquely. Its roots can be found in property law. If something is "alienable," it is exchangeable. It can be bought and sold. Alienation is thus the precondition of all private property.

---

5   On the rule of precarity and the rule of flexibility, see Guy Standing, *The Precariat: The New Dangerous Class* (London: Bloomsbury, 2011); Richard Sennett, *The Culture of the New Capitalism* (New Haven: Yale University Press, 2006); Zygmunt Bauman, *Work, Consumerism and the New Poor* (New York: Open University Press, 2005); Brett Neilson and Ned Rossiter, "Precarity as a Political Concept, or, Fordism as Exception," *Theory, Culture and Society* 25.7–8 (2008), 51–72; Kim Moody, *Workers in a Lean World: Unions in International Economy* (London: Verso, 1997); David Harvey, "Flexible Accumulation through Urbanization: Reflections on 'Post-modernism' in the American City," *Antipode* 19.3 (1987), 260–86. There are clearly differences between alienation and precarity as critical-theoretical concepts, but we do not feel that they have serious relevance for this discussion.

As a critical diagnosis of social ills, alienation is an ancient concept.[6] It was brought into social philosophy by Hegel, who saw the epic story of human development as the emergence and overcoming of spiritual alienation. His followers like the radical atheist Ludwig Feuerbach made the idea of alienation the centerpiece of an attack on religion. Humans create religion, he reasoned, and then falsely believe that religious forces rule over them. For Feuerbach, alienation meant the failure to recognize the actual extent of human agency.

Karl Marx took this abstract vision of alienation and made it concrete, historical, and political. Alienation, Marx argued, is not a symptom of existential malaise but a consequence of the organization of capitalist economies. Labor is an essential human action. Through creative work, we produce and transform the world. And in doing so, we confirm and realize our humanity and individuality. Alienation is what happens when a capitalist class captures this universal capacity to create and exploits it for its own ends.

When workers sell their labor power to others, they experience what should be a form of self-realization as "something hostile and alien" performed "under the dominion, the coercion and the yoke of another man."[7] In the alienated work

---

6   "The essence of what the prophets call 'idolatry' is not that man worships many gods instead of only one. It is that the idols are the work of man's own hands—they are things, and man bows down and worships things; worships that which he has created himself." Fromm, *Marx's Concept of Man*, 44.

7   Karl Marx, "Economic and Philosophic Manuscripts of 1844," pp. 66–125 in *The Marx–Engels Reader*, ed. Robert C. Tucker, 2nd ed. (New York: Norton, 1978), 72, 78.

process, the worker "does not affirm himself but denies himself, does not feel content but unhappy, does not develop freely his physical mind and mental energy but mortifies his body and ruins his mind."[8] Separated from their own creative capacities, alienated workers experience their time and their bodies as someone else's property. But the dehumanizing conditions in which so many people toil are not caused by immutable natural laws. They are political-economic creations. And they can be changed.

Subsequent critical thinkers developed the concept beyond the specific focus on industrial production into a general account of social alienation in class society. Now it refers "not only to powerlessness and a lack of freedom but also to a characteristic impoverishment of the relation to self and world."[9] As with Feuerbach's argument against religion, the contemporary version of alienation retains the sense that some social and political institutions have been wrongly separated out and established as superior. But now it is the market that is imagined as all-powerful. The more power that is falsely granted to economic forces, the less power do contemporary humans feel that we have.

If we apply these ideas to housing, the causes and consequences of crisis come into sharper focus. Whether we dwell in caves or in condominiums, housing is a universal human practice. Home is an extension and expression of our capacity to create. It takes an infinite variety of forms, but making a home for ourselves is an essential and universal activity. Residential alienation is what happens when a capitalist class

---

8   Ibid., 74.

9   Rahel Jaeggi, *Alienation*, trans. Frederick Neuhouser and Alan E. Smith (New York: Columbia University Press, 2014), 6.

captures the housing process and exploits it for its own ends.[10]

Hyper-commodified housing is alienated housing. It is dominated by people who see dwellings through the eyes of an investor interested in profit or a technocrat interested in control, instead of seeing it as a social right. Commodified dwelling space is not an expression of the residential needs of those who live in it. It is determined by landlords, sublessors, management companies, real estate developers, banks, bailiffs, and bureaucrats—by the ensemble of social roles and institutions that prop up the seemingly inhuman laws of housing markets in contemporary society.

In these conditions, households cannot shape their domestic environment as they wish. They do not find expression and satisfaction in their housing. They struggle to fulfill their individuality and freedom in it. Instead, their housing is the instrument of someone else's profit, and this confirms their lack of social power.

The experience of residential alienation in contemporary society, therefore, is precarity, insecurity, and disempowerment. It is fostered by commodification, displacement, and dispossession, and exacerbated by inequality. Residential

---

10 To be sure, there are some aspects of the standard account of alienation that do not apply to housing. Chief among them is the argument that alienation is a condition that emerges from industrial production rather than consumption. However, the process of housing is not pure consumerism. As many feminists have argued, residential space can only be produced through work. Home is precisely where particular forms both of production and of social reproduction occur. And without the domestic sphere, all other production would be impossible. See Silvia Federici, *Revolution at Point Zero: Housework, Reproduction and Feminist Struggle* (Oakland, CA: PM Press, 2012).

alienation represents the painful, at times traumatic, experience of a divergence between home and housing.

The thought that we want to draw from the idea of alienation is that social violence inevitably occurs when an activity that is essential to our humanity is subject to exploitation and control by others. If this is the case, residential alienation and insecurity are not symptoms of an exceptional moment of crisis. They are the widespread and predictable consequences of the place of housing within our political-economic system. They will get worse as housing becomes more commodified, as it becomes more responsive to the needs of capital and less reflective of the actual social need for residential space. They will persist in some way or another as long as the system persists in its current form.

There is nothing natural or necessary about the dehumanizing housing conditions to which millions are relegated today. Contemporary capitalist societies possess incredibly advanced technological and logistical capacities. Harnessed towards different purposes, these capacities could be used to build accessible and comfortable homes for all. But instead, market actors dominate the housing system, producing benefits for few and hardship for many. We need to understand that this state of affairs too can be changed.

Contingent Living

One only needs to listen to first-person accounts of people at risk of losing their housing to understand contemporary residential alienation.

A homeowner facing the prospect of foreclosure described the experience to researchers:

Oh the whole shock of it all. A guy who worked so many years, constantly and then everything is gone and I could be out there pushing a cart. That's unimaginable until now . . . Yes, stress, anxiety also added to the same problem that created it. You know, everything was like a catch 22, a total roller coaster going around and around.[11]

Similarly, a woman who was pushed out of her house felt shaken to her core:

Because I'm not the same person. I'm nervous all of the time, I'm always worried . . . I'm not able to pay bills sometimes, I've had my lights shut off at one period . . . It impacted every part of my life . . . I just live my life really, just living day-to-day on a survival basis . . . to be very honest, there's a part of me that will never recover from this. It took all of my security away.[12]

The pattern is repeated in many different contexts. The political economy of housing today produces anxiety, stress, and illness. The worry and shame can appear as physical symptoms. A woman whose home was repossessed described how her housing problems became embodied:

I haven't got the same energy I used to have, it drains you does this. It drains you physically and mentally. All the

---

11   Lauren M. Ross and Gregory D. Squires, "The Personal Costs of Subprime Lending and the Foreclosure Crisis: A Matter of Trust, Insecurity and Institutional Deception," *Social Science Quarterly* 92.1 (2011), 152.

12   Ibid.

worry, all the debts, everything . . . I mean since [named debt collecting agency] contacted me I've been getting chest pains. And it was when they contacted me, it was just after that I came down with the first bug.[13]

The housing system leaves many feeling like one man whose home was repossessed: "Broken, broken. Not broke money wise, but broken. Absolutely devastated."[14] For the people who make up these households, home is an unsettled place. And their experiences are shared by millions of others.

Forced mobility is one major form of residential alienation today, as the creative destruction of the built environment that is essential to the contemporary residential economy translates into insecurity and misery for households.

Due to the combination of rising housing costs, speculation, cutbacks in government programs, and stagnant wages, evictions are seeing startling growth. In many places, eviction rates are reaching historic highs. Between 2010 and 2013, evictions in San Francisco increased by 38 percent.[15] The "eviction mills" of New York City's housing court handle up to 350,000 cases per year.[16] In some years, city marshals have evicted more than 1 percent of New York's rented households, and many more

---

13   Sarah Nettleton and Roger Burrows, "When a Capital Investment Becomes an Emotional Loss: The Health Consequences of the Experience of Mortgage Possession in England," *Housing Studies* 15.3 (2000), 468.

14   Ibid., 469.

15   Shaila Dewan, "Evictions Soar in Hot Market; Renters Suffer," *New York Times*, August 24, 2014.

16   Raymond H. Brescia, "Sheltering Counsel: Towards a Right to a Lawyer in Eviction Proceedings," *Touro Law Review* 25.1 (2009), 192.

have been forced to move before that point.[17] The rise in evictions is not only a phenomenon occurring in expensive coastal housing markets. Eviction rates have also been soaring in states as disparate as Wisconsin, Kentucky, and Oklahoma.[18]

For similar reasons, evictions are increasing in other countries as well.[19] In the United Kingdom, the combination of harsh cuts to social benefits and high rental costs has meant that evictions have increased by nearly 50 percent in the past four years.[20] Across the world, megaprojects like dams or bridges, megaevents like the World Cup or the Olympics, land grabs, and resource extraction have all caused mass evictions. The 1988 Seoul Olympics resulted in the eviction of an estimated 700,000 people.[21] More than 22,000 families have already been relocated in Rio de Janeiro in advance of the 2016 Olympic Games.[22]

---

17   If anything, published data on eviction understates its prevalence, as many households are forced to move before the formal eviction process is completed.

18   See Matthew Desmond, "Unaffordable America: Poverty, Housing and Eviction," *Fast Focus* 22 (2015); Dewan, "Evictions Soar in Hot Market."

19   Sten-Åke Stenberg and Igor van Laere, "Evictions—A Hidden Social Problem: Comparative Evidence from Modern Welfare States," paper presented at the annual meeting of the International Sociological Association Research Committee 43 (2009).

20   Paul Gallagher, "Number of People Evicted from Rented Homes Has Soared since Housing Benefit Cuts Began," *The Independent*, April 13, 2015.

21   Udesh Pillay and Orli Bass, "Mega-events as a Response to Poverty Reduction: The 2010 FIFA World Cup and Its Urban Development Implications," *Urban Forum* 19 (2008), 336.

22   Bruce Dougals, "Brazil Officials Evict Families from Homes ahead of 2016 Olympic Games," *The Guardian*, October 28, 2015.

The upsurge in evictions has brought with it a wave of insecurity that is destructive for individuals and communities. Eviction represents the violent assertion of the rights of property owners over the needs of inhabitants. The mere threat of being evicted is one of the ways in which landlords exercise power over tenants. Housing researchers have demonstrated that eviction is a traumatizing experience. Evictees are forced to reconstitute social and professional networks in circumstances that almost by definition are strained. Some evicted families go separate ways and split up. The experience of losing one's home, and the loss of many of one's personal possessions, creates fear, stigma, and anxiety. A number of studies have shown that for some people, being evicted leads directly to homelessness.[23] One study comparing single mothers who have been evicted with those who have not found that the evictees experienced higher rates of depression, other negative health consequences for themselves and their families, and further economic hardship—consequences that were still being felt two years after being forced to move.[24]

The alienating impact of foreclosure is similar to that of

---

23   See Elizabeth A. Mulroy and Terry S. Lane, "Housing Affordability, Stress and Single Mothers: Pathway to Homelessness," *Journal of Sociology and Social Welfare* 19.3 (2015), 51–64; Chester Hartman and David Robinson, "Evictions: The Hidden Housing Problem," *Housing Policy Debate* 14.4 (2003), 461–501; Martha Burt, "Homeless Families, Singles, and Others: Findings from the 1996 National Survey of Homeless Assistance Providers and Clients," *Housing Policy Debate* 12.4 (2001), 737–80.

24   Matthew Desmond and Rachel Tolbert Kimbro, "Eviction's Fallout: Housing, Hardship and Health," *Social Forces* (forthcoming), 1–30; Matthew Desmond, "Eviction and the Reproduction of Urban Poverty," *American Journal of Sociology* 118.1 (2012), 88–133.

eviction. Eviction may be instigated by a landlord and foreclosure by a lender, but they are two versions of the same story of dispossession.

As with evictions, foreclosures are not concentrated in expensive coastal cities but distributed throughout the United States, affecting households in urban, suburban, and rural areas, and middle-class as well as working-class and poor households.[25] Like eviction, foreclosure represents the domination of the exchange value of housing over its use value, with similarly alienating consequences. The "radical risk" experienced by homeowners under threat of foreclosure is physically and psychologically destabilizing.[26] Poor health, both physical and mental, is often a trigger for foreclosure, and the foreclosure process itself can worsen health problems. Brought on by stress, anxiety, and fear, residential insecurity can manifest as medical symptoms.[27] Communities with increasing numbers of

25 Adam Wodka, "Landscapes of Foreclosure: The Foreclosure Crisis in Rural America" (Washington, DC: NeighborWorks America, 2009); Christopher Niedt and William Martin, "Who Are the Foreclosed? A Statistical Portrait of America in Crisis," *Housing Policy Debate* 23.1 (2013), 159–76.

26 Susan Saegert, Desiree Fields, and Kimberly Libman, "Deflating the Dream: Radical Risk and the Neoliberalization of Homeownership," *Journal of Urban Affairs* 31.3 (2009), 297–317.

27 Kimberly Libman, Desiree Fields, and Susan Saegert, "Housing and Health: A Social Ecological Perspective on the US Foreclosure Crisis," *Housing, Theory and Society* 29.1 (2012), 1–24; Theresa L. Osypuk, Cleopatra Howard Caldwell, Robert W. Platt, and Dawn P. Misra, "The Consequences of Foreclosure for Depressive Symptomatology," *Annals of Epidemiology* 22.6 (2012), 379–87; D. J. Pevalin, "Housing Repossessions, Evictions and Common Mental Illness in the UK: Results from a Household Panel

foreclosures tend to exhibit spikes in the prevalence of mental health problems, an association that is stronger in poorer areas and in communities of color.[28]

Whether caused by eviction, foreclosure, urban renewal, gentrification, or other sources, the experience of displacement can be devastating. In "Grieving for a Lost Home," a classic essay exploring the pain of dislocation, Marc Fried records some of his research subjects' reactions to their forced move from the working-class West End of Boston:

> "I felt as though I had lost everything," "I felt like my heart was taken out of me," "I felt like taking the gaspipe," "I lost all the friends I knew," "I always felt I had to go home to the West End and even now I feel like crying when I pass by," "Something of me went with the West End," "I felt cheated," "What's the use of thinking about it . . . I threw up a lot," "I had a nervous breakdown."[29]

Fried's account is echoed by the psychiatrist and housing researcher Mindy Fullilove, who identifies displacement with what she calls "root shock . . . the traumatic stress reaction to

---

Study," *Journal of Epidemiology and Community Health* 63.11 (2009), 949–51.

28   Jason N. Houle, "Mental Health in the Foreclosure Crisis," *Social Science and Medicine* 118 (2014), 1–8.

29   Marc Fried, "Grieving for a Lost Home," pp. 359–79 in James Q. Wilson, ed., *Urban Renewal: The Record and the Controversy* (Cambridge, MA: MIT Press, 1966), 360. See also Herbert Gans, *The Urban Villagers: Group and Class in the Life of Italian-Americans* (New York: Free Press, 1962).

the destruction of all or part of one's emotional ecosystem."[30] This trauma is produced as a matter of routine in the contemporary housing system.

The Experience of Insecurity

Residential alienation above all manifests as insecurity. As such, it aggravates struggles in other areas of life. When housing is insecure, people stay in jobs that they would prefer to quit. Or they are compelled to take on second or third jobs. Housing insecurity makes some people stay in unhappy or abusive relationships, and prevents other families from living together. Workers are forced to endure grueling commutes. Children's lives are destabilized and schooling is interrupted.

According to an English housing charity, one in three adults reports that housing is causing stress and depression in their households. One in four reports increased arguments with family members due to housing costs.[31] When housing is a struggle, normal anxiety and daily adversities become magnified. The sense of being ground down can become overwhelming.

Many households feel anxiety about their housing today. But for the poorest, residential precarity is destabilizing on a deep level. One of the ways that housing researchers understand the experience of alienation and disalienation in dwelling is through

---

30 Mindy Fullilove, *Root Shock: How Tearing Up City Neighborhoods Hurts America, and What We Can Do about It* (New York: One World/Ballantine Books, 2004), 11.

31 Shelter England, "Housing Costs Cause Stress and Depression for Millions," January 17, 2013.

the concept of "ontological security,"[32] which was first proposed by the Scottish psychiatrist R. D. Laing. Ontological security is the sense that the stability of the world can be taken for granted. It is the emotional foundation that allows us to feel at ease in our environment and at home in our housing. Ontological security is a subjective state, but it depends upon a number of structural conditions. It presupposes stable access to dwelling space that is under the resident's own control. It assumes a particular class position, which makes the steady reproduction of everyday life possible. It also implies a functioning domestic economy, which invariably raises questions about gender roles and the remuneration of labor. It is underpinned by legal rights that maintain the sanctity of the home as the domain of personal sovereignty. It is, in essence, the psychosocial corollary to full political and social citizenship—and as such has long been reserved as an elite, male, white privilege.

For poor households, the current housing system seems designed specifically to produce residential alienation instead of ontological security.

Homelessness may represent the most extreme form of residential alienation. On the street or in shelters, homeless individuals and families are denied housing security. The unhoused

---

32   R. D. Laing, *The Divided Self: An Existential Study in Sanity and Madness* (London: Pelican, 1965); see also Deborah K. Padgett, "There's No Place Like (a) Home: Ontological Security among Persons with Serious Mental Illness in the United States," *Social Science and Medicine* 64 (2007), 1925–36; Rosemary Hiscock, Ade Kearns, Sally MacIntyre, and Anne Ellaway, "Ontological Security and Psycho-social Benefits from the Home: Qualitative Evidence on Issues of Tenure," *Housing, Theory and Society* 18.1–2 (2001), 50–66; Anthony Giddens, *Modernity and Self-Identity: Self and Society in the Late Modern Age* (Cambridge: Polity, 1991).

are subject to violence at the hands of strangers and the police, and are excluded from the social rights that derive from place of residence. Homeless people do develop strategies for coping with and resisting their marginality. But unable to draw on stable housing as a resource, they do so in spite of their residential situation.

Homelessness is not some quirk of urban life—it is a major segment of the housing system. Whereas in the past the homeless were predominantly single men, modern homelessness is a family phenomenon. Families comprise nearly 80 percent of the population in the New York City shelter system. In the past year in New York alone, 42,000 children were unhoused for at least one night.[33] Modern homelessness reflects the instability of low-income housing. Cuts to social services, disappearing rent regulations, shrinking public housing programs, and gentrification all contribute to it.[34]

---

33 Coalition for the Homeless, "Turning the Tide: New York City Takes Steps to Combat Record Homelessness, but Albany Must Step Up" (2015), 2. For an analysis of the experience of fixity and mobility among homeless youth in London, see Emma Jackson, "Fixed in Mobility: Young Homeless People and the City," *International Journal of Urban and Regional Research* 36.4 (2012), 725–41.

34 On gentrification's link to homelessness, see Institute for Children, Poverty and Homelessness, "The Process of Poverty Destabilization: How Gentrification Is Reshaping Upper Manhattan and the Bronx and Increasing Homelessness in New York City" (2014); Institute for Children and Poverty, "Pushed Out: The Hidden Costs of Gentrification: Displacement and Homelessness" (2009); Peter Marcuse, "Gentrification, Homelessness, and the Work Process: Housing Markets and Labour Markets in the Quartered City," *Housing Studies* 4.3 (1989), 211–20.

Those who are not homeless but who occupy places on the bottom rungs of the housing hierarchy are also subject to residential insecurity, and may have spent time homeless themselves.[35] This includes the uncountable numbers of people barely holding on to their places of residence: those who have doubled up with friends and relatives, families sleeping in temporary quarters like hostels, and other informal and short-term strategies.[36]

Precarity can be found in other segments of the low-income housing market. The unregulated world of illegal conversions has been called New York's "housing underground."[37] It

35   Dennis P. Culhane, Chang-Moo Lee, and Susan M. Wachter, "Where the Homeless Come from: A Study of the Prior Address Distribution of Families Admitted to Public Shelters in New York City and Philadelphia," *Housing Policy Debate* 7.2 (1996), 327–65.

36   Marguerite V. Marin and Edward F. Vacha, "Self-Help Strategies and Resources among People at Risk of Homelessness: Empirical Findings and Social Services Policy," *Social Work* 39.6 (1994), 649–57; Edward F. Vacha and Marguerite V. Marin, "Doubling Up: Low Income Households Sheltering the Hidden Homeless," *Journal of Sociology and Social Work* 20.3 (1993), 25–41. On the importance of residential hotels and their disappearance, see Brian J. Sullivan and Jonathan Burke, "Single-Room Occupancy Housing in New York City: The Origins and Dimensions of a Crisis," *CUNY Law Review* 17 (2013), 901–31; Terri Wingate-Lewinson, June Gary Hopps, and Patricia Reeves, "Liminal Living at an Extended Stay Hotel: Feeling 'Stuck' in a Housing Situation," *Journal of Sociology and Social Welfare* 37.2 (2010), 9–34.

37   Pratt Center for Community Development and Chhaya Community Development Corporation, *New York's Housing Underground: A Refuge and Resource* (New York: Pratt Center and Chhaya CDC, 2008).

accounts for an estimated 4 percent of the city's housing stock, providing residential quarters for up to half a million people, or one out of every twenty-five New Yorkers.[38] Most of these apartments are not located downtown. They are concentrated in suburban areas of outer boroughs, and in the borough of Queens in particular, which is thought to be home to nearly three-quarters of such apartments. Tens of thousands of basements and rooms in Long Island and other suburbs have also been converted into illegal apartments.[39] Most other metropolitan areas contain similar sectors.

These units provide a crucial resource for low-income New Yorkers, especially recent immigrants. But they are risky places to live. They tend to be overcrowded, shoddily constructed, and relatively expensive. And as events like the Woodycrest Avenue fire show, they are dangerous. Three people were killed in a fire in an illegal conversion in Woodside in 2009. That same weekend a man died in a fire in an unregulated boarding house in Cypress Hills.[40] Five people were killed and a baby's skull was fractured in a 2010 fire in an illegally converted apartment building in Bensonhurst, for which landlords were later arraigned for manslaughter.[41] In 2013, a landlord in Jackson Heights was charged with a number of crimes including reckless endangerment for placing nearly fifty people in underground

38   Ibid.

39   Vivian S. Toy, "Unraveling the Issue of Illegal Apartments," *New York Times*, June 8, 2003.

40   Kareem Fahim, "4 Are Killed in 2 Fires in Queens and Brooklyn," *New York Times*, November 7, 2009.

41   Andy Newman and Mosi Secret, "Manslaughter Charges for Landlords in Brooklyn Fire That Killed 5," *New York Times*, June 14, 2012.

apartments with poorly installed utilities, illegal subdivisions, and inadequate fire exits. One of his tenants, Fernando Camano, paid $1,400 a month for an illegally converted three-bedroom basement apartment that he shared with his wife, his three children, and two boarders. He told a reporter, "It never ever felt safe."[42] Never feeling safe in one's home is the essence of ontological insecurity.

An alienating domestic environment is the predictable result of landlords strategically under-maintaining their buildings. Monsignor John Powis, a priest and activist, said of a Bushwick building left in a state of ruin by its owner, a firm named Fast Money Now LLC, "I don't know what's worse, living there or the shelter."[43] Community organizers describe the interior of a similar Bushwick house:

> The air hangs heavy from mold and decay, causing shortness of breath and other respiratory problems such as asthma. Rodents gnaw through the walls while roaches and roach traps are omnipresent figures on countertops, tables, walls and floors. Light fixtures and electrical sockets are rusty from leaking ceilings and walls, exposing residents to electrical shocks and electrocution. The paint and floors reveal their many layers, the result of landlord neglect.[44]

In buildings like this, complaints go unanswered. Requests for

---

42   Sarah Maslin Nir, "Landlord Accused of Endangering Tenants," *New York Times*, March 27, 2013.

43   David Gonzalez, "Brooklyn Holdouts Battle Their Landlord," *New York Times*, September 29, 2008.

44   Make the Road by Walking, *This Side of Poverty: Bushwick's Housing Crisis* (New York: Make the Road by Walking, Inc., 2003), 6.

repairs are ignored. When landlords do eventually decide to maintain such buildings in order to exploit new market opportunities, they jack up the rent and send their low-income tenants packing.

Low-income living is difficult enough. But the feeling of alienation is intensified by the social stigma that outside observers apply to housing that differs from the imagined middle-class suburban ideal. One resident of a public housing development described the experience of stigmatization: people who do not live in public housing "don't even have to know you as a person, but as soon as you tell them where you live, they think bad of you . . . you're dirty, you're sub-human, you're poor."[45] The disgrace that comes from living in stigmatized locations and housing types is a form of symbolic class violence, adding a layer of socially generated shame to living conditions that may already be precarious.[46]

---

45   Lynne C. Manzo, Rachel G. Kleit, and Dawn Couch, "'Moving Three Times Is Like Having Your House on Fire Once': The Experience of Place and Impeding Displacement among Public Housing Residents," *Urban Studies* 45.9 (2008), 1865.

46   On territorial stigmatization, see Tom Slater, "Territorial Stigmatization: Symbolic Defamation and the Contemporary Metropolis," in John Hannigan and Greg Richards, eds, *The Handbook of New Urban Studies* (London: SAGE, forthcoming); Hamish Kallin and Tom Slater, "Activating Territorial Stigma: Gentrifying Marginality on Edinburgh's Periphery," *Environment and Planning A* 46.6 (2014), 1351–68; Lynn Hancock and Gerry Mooney, "'Welfare Ghettos' and the 'Broken Society': Territorial Stigmatization in the Contemporary UK," *Housing, Theory and Society* 30.1 (2013), 46–64; David Garbin and Gareth Millington, "Territorial Stigma and the Politics of Resistance in a Parisian *Banlieue*: La Courneuve and Beyond," *Urban Studies* 49.10 (2012), 2067–83; Loïc Wacquant, "Territorial Stigmatization in the Age of Marginality," *Thesis Eleven* 91.1 (2007), 66–77.

In America, the narrative that housing is the key to dignity and stability is deeply ingrained. But in most times and places, it has only described the experience of elites. Ontological security has only ever been offered provisionally to poor people, to female-headed households, and to households of color.[47] The freedom to reside without great difficulty or fear, to establish a household as a space of psychological and economic stability with relative ease, is today a form of privilege.

Ownership and the Alienation of Property

The standard response to residential alienation by the political and economic establishment is to reassert the psychological and social superiority of homeownership. From James Madison's declaration that "the Freeholders of the country would be the safest depositories of Republican liberty"[48] to Barack Obama's praise for "responsible homeownership" as "the most tangible cornerstone that lies at the heart of the American Dream,"[49] American political history is not lacking for tributes to private ownership of housing. And the national myths of other countries are often based around similar narratives.

---

47 For a sharp analysis of working-class women's experience of feeling "homeless at home," see Katy Bennett, "Homeless at Home in East Durham," *Antipode* 43.4 (2011), 960–85.

48 Cited in *The Debates in the Federal Convention of 1787 Which Framed the Constitution of the United States of America: Reported by James Madison*, ed. Gaillard Hunt and James Brown Scott (New York: Oxford University Press, 1920), 353.

49 President Barack Obama, "Remarks by the President on Responsible Homeownership," press release, August 6, 2013.

Homeownership is presented as the antidote to alienation, an automatic source of residential satisfaction and ontological security. A 1971 position paper published by the British government summed up this position: "Home ownership . . . satisfies a deep and natural desire on the part of the householder to have independent control of the home that shelters him and his family."[50] The businessman and US senator Charles Percy expressed this sentiment in pure form in a campaign speech:

> a man who owns his own home acquires with it a new dignity. He begins to take pride in what is his own, and pride in conserving and improving it for his children. He becomes a more steadfast and concerned citizen of his community. He becomes more self-confident and self-reliant. The mere act of becoming a homeowner transforms him. It gives him roots, a sense of belonging, a true stake in his community and its well-being.[51]

Homeownership here is cast as a magical form of tenure that "transforms" the occupant. For Percy, as for many of today's politicians and housing campaigners, private ownership of housing is not just a method for the provision of dwelling space.

---

50   Cited in Jim Kemeny, "A Critique of Homeownership," pp. 272–95 in Rachel G. Bratt, Chester Hartman, and Ann Meyerson, eds, *Critical Perspectives on Housing* (Philadelphia: Temple University Press, 1986), 272.

51   Senator Charles Percy, "A New Dawn for Our Cities," campaign address, Chicago, September 15, 1966, printed in *Congressional Record*, October 16, 1966. During his political career, Percy was a major promoter of homeownership initiatives as solutions to the housing problem.

It is a form of empowerment, a marker of dignity, and a way to overcome social isolation and estrangement.

Is homeownership in fact the solution to residential alienation? The alienating effect of the direct control of one's home by an outsider is hard to deny. The petty landlord, the unresponsive management company, the absentee owner, and the arbitrary government employee personify the problem. To live in someone else's house is to live in alienated housing, in the straightforward legal sense as well as in the psychosocial sense. It does not take much research or argument to convince us that living under the control of another is neither comfortable nor secure.

But the relationship between residential alienation and housing tenure is not so simple. First of all, ownership is a complex social and legal concept. Ownership is far from the type of absolute status that we have in mind with phrases such as "a man's home is his castle." It is in fact the creature, and subject to the whims, of public policy, governmental action, neighborhood changes, economic conditions, city budgets, insurance rates and regulations, bank policies, social standards, and technological developments, among other things. It includes a bundle of rights, powers, privileges, and immunities that differ in different places and times.[52] The mere switch from a lease to a deed does not in itself necessarily provide a greater bundle of rights to the owner than a tenant may have. A solid lease with strong legal protections can easily provide a tenant with more security than an owner might receive from a deed subject to a

---

52   James Barlow and Simon Duncan, "The Use and Abuse of Housing Tenure," *Housing Studies* 3.4 (1988), 219–31; Peter Marcuse, "The Legal Attributes of Homeownership for Low and Moderate Income Families," Working Paper 209-1-1 (Washington, DC: Urban Institute, 1972).

heavy mortgage under many conditions. In many places, the legal situation for tenants has been tilted towards less security, but the balance could in principle be tilted back.

The most important attributes of the tenure relationship are in fact more affected by the characteristics of the occupant and of the society in which ownership occurs. Safety within one's home, for instance, which as we have said is a crucial precondition for ontological security, will be more determined by the attitude of the police towards an occupant than by the contents of the deed to the occupant's house. Public services, legislation governing occupancy rights, neighborhood characteristics, and above all the distribution of wealth, the nature of housing law, and access to social security are far more important than the form of tenure.

Second, the economic and social benefits of homeownership are easily overstated. The correlation between class status and tenure has varied widely historically and between different countries.[53] The economic advantages of the homeowner are much less substantial or secure than many assume. In some countries, ownership includes tax benefits, but these are creations of policy that can easily be changed or eliminated and not effects of tenure itself.

As is known all too well by the millions who have recently lost their homes to foreclosure, ownership is no guarantee of stability. Without a steady income to meet mortgage payments, or if anything interrupts the ability to work, ownership is a route to catastrophe. One woman in mortgage distress told researchers: "I stay in my room a lot. I really don't have any

---

53 See Richard Harris and Chris Hamnett, "The Myth of the Promised Land: The Social Diffusion of Home Ownership in Britain and North America," *Annals of the Association of American Geographers* 77.2 (1987), 173–90.

friends that I socialized with, and I don't go out a lot, and I'm always thinking about, 'What if I don't have my home, I'm on the street.'"[54] Another homeowner facing problems meeting her debt obligations expressed similar sentiments:

> Emotionally, I tell you, I wanted to kill myself. I wanted to blow my brains out, just an easy way to get out of everything, you know, because it was too much. One person can't handle a lot of things, and I'm telling you when you're under emotional stress, pain don't go away.[55]

For these women, it is clear that homeownership was not the antidote to residential alienation. It was the cause of it.

It is true that some research confirms the coincidence of homeownership and a number of measures of physical and psychosocial health. But other studies have shown that no greater emotional security or health benefits stem from ownership specifically.[56] Rather, those who are wealthier tend to feel more secure, and they also tend to be

---

54   Danya E. Keene, Sarah K. Cowan, and Amy Castro Baker, "'When You're in a Crisis Like That, You Don't Want People to Know': Mortgage Strain, Stigma, and Mental Health," *American Journal of Public Health* 105.5 (2015), 1010.

55   Ibid.

56   Reinout Kleinhans and Marja Elsinga, "'Buy Your Home and Feel in Control': Does Home Ownership Achieve the Empowerment of Former Tenants of Social Housing?," *European Journal of Housing Policy* 10.1 (2010), 41–61; Hiscock et al., "Ontological Security and Psycho-social Benefits from the Home"; Ade Kearns, Rosemary Hiscock, Anne Ellaway, and Sally Macintyre, "'Beyond Four Walls.' The Psycho-social Benefits of Home: Evidence from West Central Scotland," *Housing Studies* 15.3 (2000); 387–410.

homeowners. There is nothing magical about ownership as a form of tenure.

The idea that homeowners make better neighbors and community members is a combination of class prejudice and myth.[57] Homeownership today often occurs in highly exclusionary contexts like condominiums and gated communities that are specifically designed to prevent encounters with others. And as house flipping and speculation demonstrate, private ownership can be far more temporary than renting.

The economic aspect of homeownership appeals to a narrowly instrumental logic that is ultimately indifferent to the fate of the wider community. If a house is just an investment, then its value hinges on what its owner can get for it and is independent of his or her relationship with neighbors. A housing shortage or overcrowding in the neighborhood may be exactly what a small-scale real estate capitalist would most like to see.

Finally, homeownership is inextricable from the broader system of inequality and private property that produces social and residential alienation in the first place. The outsiders in control may be banks or seemingly disembodied "market forces," but they are in control nonetheless. In an unequal, hyper-commodified world, owner-occupied housing can be alienated housing too.

Homeownership does not overcome the division between exchange value and use value that is the foundation of alienation. Increasing it cannot solve the housing problem. The potential for some to make riches from property ownership still depends on the impoverishment of others. And we see that countries with a stronger dedication to private ownership, like

---

57   See Stephanie M. Stern, "Reassessing the Citizen Virtues of Homeownership," *Columbia Law Review* 100.2 (2011), 101–51.

the United States or the United Kingdom, do not have more humane housing systems than countries like Germany or Switzerland that have relatively more renters. Research suggests that countries tilted towards private ownership have less humane housing systems.[58]

In considering the extent of alienation in bourgeois society, Marx argues that

> the possessing class and the proletarian class represent one and the same human self-alienation. But the former feels satisfied and affirmed in this self-alienation, experiences the alienation as a sign *of its own power*, and possesses in it the *appearance* of a human existence. The latter, however, feels destroyed in this alienation, seeing in it its own impotence and the reality of an inhuman existence.[59]

We can make a similar argument regarding housing. Middle-class professionals who own their housing might seem to have

---

58   See research by Jim Kemeny and others regarding the relationships between tenure and welfare, e.g., Jim Kemeny, "'The Really Big Trade-Off' between Home Ownership and Welfare: Castles' Evaluation of the 1980 Thesis, and a Reformulation 25 Years On," *Housing, Theory and Society* 22.2 (2005), 59–75; Kemeny, "Comparative Housing and Welfare: Theorising the Relationship," *Journal of Housing and the Built Environment* 16.1 (2001), 53–70; Francis G. Castles, "The Really Big Trade-Off: Home Ownership and the Welfare State in the New World and the Old," *Acta Politica* 33 (1998), 5–19.

59   Karl Marx, "Alienation and Social Classes" (excerpted from *The Holy Family: A Critique of Critical Criticism*, 1845), pp. 133–5 in *The Marx–Engels Reader*, 133, emphasis in original.

escaped the alienation experienced by the insecure tenant who is subjected to the arbitrary whims of a landlord. Middle-class homeowners may feel that their residential situation reflects their talents and achievements. But they are still living within an inhumane housing system—they have simply used their resources to construct a more livable corner within it. As we have seen, this solidity could melt in an instant. And their position is more reflective of their place in an unequal social structure than anything having to do with either their personal virtues or their housing.

Rich households are more likely than others to own property rather than to rent it. There are reasons for this, but they have nothing to do with the effects of housing tenure per se. Housing is one investment among many that are typically made by the wealthy. Property owners use their housing strategically in a competitive economy and as a replacement for pensions and other forms of social security that have been eroded. And in societies ruled by property-owning classes, property ownership will obviously be privileged.

In other words, homeownership patterns are both expressions and instruments of inequality. Increasing homeownership without ending inequality is not a route to ending alienation. It will just lead to more debt and more insecurity.

None of this is to deny that insecure tenancy can be a distinctly miserable experience, especially in perilous times. But it is to deny that homeownership is the way to lessen residential alienation throughout society.

In the end, there is no simple relationship between tenure and alienation in housing. Tenancy can be a particularly precarious experience, especially in a commodified, financialized housing regime. But homeownership can be just as grueling and exploitative. To claim that the mere act of becoming a homeowner is transformative and that it is therefore the solution to the housing problem is not only wrong—it is pernicious.

Imagining Residential Disalienation

Many Americans justify the untrammeled rule of free markets by reference to some sacred, if often under-specified, ideal of freedom. But giving market actors increased control over housing has led to the steady erasure of the freedom to dwell how and where one desires.

The housing problem today needs to be understood in its proper human context. A truly humane housing system would measure its success or failure not in home prices or the number of mega-mansions but in the extent to which the residential good life is actually provided for everyone. For all of the ideological significance of home and family values in American politics, neither liberalism nor conservatism has ever articulated a politics of home in this sense.[60]

As with many areas of contemporary life, one person's crisis is another's business opportunity. The real estate industry is intent on selling lifestyle as a solution to residential alienation and status anxiety. Countless television shows and magazines exist with the sole purpose of promoting the dream that home improvement is the essence of personal fulfillment. As we have seen, the cult of domestic consumerism is part and parcel of a larger ideology of private property and national destiny. But it is not possible to consume one's way out of alienation, because

---

60   Peter Marcuse, "The Liberal/Conservative Divide in the History of Housing Policy in the United States," *Housing Studies* 16.6 (2001), 717–36.

under-consumption is not the basis of alienation. The basis of alienation is the system that treats housing and the rest of human experience as commodities.

Just as the idea of brokenness contains within it the prospect of wholeness, an account of alienation, Ernest Mandel reminds us, "implies and contains a theory of disalienation."[61] What, then, would residential disalienation look like? What would need to change for everyone to feel at home in their housing?

Alienation may be rooted deep in the contemporary political economy, but the disalienation, democratization, and humanization of the housing system are still meaningful demands. Disalienation would mean reorganizing the housing system around the goal of providing residential stability and ontological security for all. Changing the housing system in this way would require legal changes to bolster the relative position of residents over landlords and banks, for example by weakening the ability to evict residents or requiring that foreclosed home-owners have the option to stay in their homes as regulated, secure tenants. It would require expanding the role of public, nonprofit, and collective tenures. It would mean putting tenants and residents in control of their housing and decisions that affect them.

To demand the disalienation of housing would be to demand something that is itself alien to the housing system under neoliberal capitalism: that housing be produced not in order to make money but in order to provide decent places for everyone to live.

---

61   Ernest Mandel, "The Causes of Alienation," pp. 13–30 in Ernest Mandel and George Novack, *The Marxist Theory of Alienation: Three Essays* (New York: Pathfinder Press, 1973), 30.

3

Oppression and Liberation in Housing

Langdon Post, the first chairman of the New York City Housing Authority, understood the housing question in the widest terms. "Let us face the facts squarely," he wrote in 1936. "All revolutions are germinated in the slums; every riot is a slum riot . . . As I see it, it is a question of housing—or else."[1] Post was a reformist seeking to gain the support of New York's political and financial establishment. He saw public housing as a necessary intervention to reduce suffering, but also as a way to manage conflict and forestall insurrection.

Housing is always more than just housing. It provides shelter, but fulfills other functions as well. Among the most important of these nonresidential roles is that housing is an instrument for politics, and not only in tense moments of crisis like 1930s New York. In all social settings, dwelling space structures power relations. It can be used to maintain the social order, or to support challenges to it. Neither existing residential patterns

---

1   Langdon W. Post, *Housing . . . Or Else: A Letter to a Banker* (New York: New York City Housing Authority, 1936), 22.

nor possibilities for future change can be understood without looking at the ways in which housing is part and parcel of social and political struggles.

The political dimension of housing is something that both liberal and conservative commentators tend to miss. There are two standard approaches to understanding residential problems today. Both remove the elements of politics and social struggle from the housing question.

One tendency is to acknowledge the existence of residential problems but to cast them as the special concerns of particular populations that are ill-housed, in the context of an overall housing system that is held to be functioning well.[2] It focuses on the characteristics of people imagined as exceptional groups: chiefly the poor, the elderly, ethnic minorities, and single-parent households, and seeks ways to integrate them into the existing housing market. At best, this approach conceals the general systemic failures of housing under a collection of separate and individual problems. At worst, it blames the victim.

The other common approach reduces housing to economics. In its crude form, it explains the lack of adequate housing as a function of supply and effective demand.[3] This position

---

2   Peter Marcuse, "The Pitfalls of Specialism: Special Groups and the General Problem of Housing," pp. 76–82 in Chester Hartman and Sara Rosenberry, eds, *Housing Issues of the 1990s* (Westport, CT: Praeger, 1988).

3   For example: "Many observers claim that we are in the midst of an 'affordable housing shortage' or, even worse, an 'affordable housing crisis.' The primary concern is that too many households live in 'unaffordable' rental units . . . [W]e conclude that a shortage of income is largely behind the housing affordability problem despite the current focus on housing." See Ron Feldman, "The Affordable Housing Shortage: Considering the Problem, Causes

holds that if only developers were freer to build, or if only everyone had higher wages, the housing problem would automatically be solved. The solution either way is just "growth" that leaves the housing system and the broader political economy as they are. Some radical urban analysts risk making a similar mistake and reducing the housing question to the economics of shelter.[4]

Both of these interpretations leave many aspects of actually existing housing patterns unexplained: for example, the persistence of racial segregation, the gender bias of housing design, the strengths and limitations of tenant organizing, or the full ideological significance of the glorification of homeownership. These all have bearing on the economic and physical dimensions of housing units. But they cannot be reduced to them. They relate, instead, to the social antagonisms at the heart of capitalist societies. They require an analysis of the housing system in the broader contexts of class power, racism, patriarchy, and other forms of structural violence.

To say that housing is political is to say that struggles over dwelling space are inextricable from conflicts over power, resources, autonomy, and agency. Housing is not only a question of who occupies what building, and it is not only shaped by the direct interest of housing suppliers in pursuit of profit. It is also formed by conflicts between classes, institutions, and the state, and used by these groups in struggles with one another.

---

and Solutions," Banking and Policy Working Paper 02-02 (Minneapolis: Federal Reserve Bank of Minneapolis, 2002), 2.

4   See, e.g., some of the criticisms in Todd Swanstrom, "Beyond Economism: Urban Political Economy and the Postmodern Challenge," *Journal of Urban Affairs* 15.1 (1993), 55–78.

Housing will always be political one way or another. The point is to recognize, critique and change the goals towards which it is mobilized. We need to understand how dwelling space can be used in oppressive ways—and develop alternatives that unlock housing's emancipatory potential.

Residential Oppression

Housing can provide the material basis for oppression, domination, and inequality. The idea of residential oppression points to the link between the provision of housing and the power to rule. The concept of housing oppression refers to systematic efforts to use place and quality of residence in order to enhance political stability, to intensify exploitation, to undermine resistance, to impose cultural uniformity, or to shore up the legitimacy of a prevailing system. It highlights that aspect of housing that circumscribes opportunities, that dictates roles, that inhibits protest, that produces conformity, that undermines resistance, that integrates households into a hierarchical social system.

Oppression is not simply the result of the system of private provision of housing for profit. For many, and particularly for the poor, that system does indeed result in bad housing, even oppressively bad housing. Such ill-housing, however, requires no additional concept of oppression to explain it.

The oppressive functions of residential space coexist with the commodity form but are not purely a matter of economic exchange. The potential for oppression stems from the distinctive aspects of housing as a commodity and the importance of its use. Many of these aspects are well known. Housing is the most durable and expensive of consumer goods. It involves land and location to an exceptional degree. Its provision cannot be reduced below established standards without serious personal and social consequences.[5]

Yet housing is also different from other commodities because it uniquely helps to structure social life. Of course other commodities have this extra-economic aspect also. For example, clothing and jewelry are as much signifiers of identity as they are protection against the elements or a tribute to conceptions of beauty; cars can be status symbols as well as means of transportation. But housing is a major determinant of one's access to social resources perhaps more than any other commodity. Housing preeminently creates and reinforces connections between people, communities, and institutions, and thus it ultimately creates relationships of power. That it is used in this way does not make a house any less a commodity. But it means that housing must be considered as more than just a mere commodity if its production, distribution, and use are to be understood—or changed.

One of the major oppressive uses of housing is to bolster the exploitation of labor.[6] As could be seen in the design of towns like Pullman, Illinois, now part of Chicago, or in Alfred Krupp's domination of Essen in the Ruhr Valley, company towns reflected the desire to control all aspects of workers' lives. Workers' colonies (so called by their owners) were designed to promote a "healthy, satisfied, settled, and loyal breed of

---

5   See various contributions to Rachel G. Bratt, Chester Hartman, and Ann Meyerson, eds, *Critical Perspectives on Housing* (Philadelphia, PA: Temple University Press, 1986).

6   As we explained in chapter one, the interweaving of housing with the exploitation of labor was the norm in pre-commodified settings; and such practices did not end with the rise of commodified housing, but rather exist alongside it.

workers." But in these settlements, surveillance was paramount, and the ever-present threat of eviction effectively undercut the ability of workers to organize.[7]

Krupp's Essen seems downright pleasant compared to the workers' dormitories found today in the Gulf countries, the Pearl River delta, and elsewhere. Labor camps like Sonapar on the outskirts of Dubai provide housing for the migrant construction workers building the luxury skyscrapers and tourist attractions in the center of town. In labor camps, residential space facilitates exploitation by impeding resistance and exerting constant control over workers stripped of rights and autonomy.[8] Laborers sleep in bunk beds in rooms housing as many as twenty men. In some camps, food and other necessities are only

---

7 Michael Weisser, "Arbeiterkolonien: Über Motive zum Bau von Arbeitersiedlungen durch industrielle Unternehmener im 19. und frühen 20. Jahrhundert in Deutschland," pp. 7–56 in Joachim Petsch, ed, *Architektur und Städtebau im 20. Jahrhundert*, vol. 2 (West Berlin: Verlag für das Studium der Arbeiterbewegung, 1975); Gwendolyn Wright, *Building the Dream: A Social History of Housing in America* (Cambridge, MA: MIT Press, 1983), 58–72; J. D. Porteous, "The Nature of the Company Town," *Transactions of the Institute of British Geographers* 51 (1970), 127–42; Stanley Buder, "The Model Town of Pullman: Town Planning and Social Control in the Gilded Age," *Journal of the American Institute of Planners* 33.1 (1967), 2–10.

8 Michelle Buckley, "Locating Neoliberalism in Dubai: Migrant Workers and Class Struggle in the Autocratic City," *Antipode* 45.2 (2013), 256–74; Ahmed Kanna, "Dubai in a Jagged World," *Middle East Report* 243 (2007), 22–9; Irene Eng, "The Rise of Manufacturing Towns: Externally Driven Industrialization and Urban Development in the Pearl River Delta of China," *International Journal of Urban and Regional Research* 21.4 (1997), 554–68.

available from company canteens. Leisure and social activities are banned. Movement is closely controlled. Bosses confiscate workers' passports. Compounds can become virtual prisons to prevent workers from complaining about routine violations.[9] Such direct exploitation is not the only oppressive function of housing. In other cases, housing can be made to serve a more general function of social repression. National and municipal leaders have sought to control troublesome populations by separating, concentrating, or redesigning their housing, so that they can be more easily monitored. The most famous example is Baron Haussmann's destruction of working-class quarters of Second Empire Paris. Haussmann sought to negate the use of residential neighborhoods as seats of resistance. He ensured the elimination of narrow streets that could be barricaded and their replacement with barracks and plazas that were more easily controlled. One witness discussing the militarized Place de la République observed, "It would be a dangerous spot for any subversive ideas that might take their chance here."[10]

State-led rebuilding efforts in cities across the world today carry echoes of Haussmann's revenge upon the *les classes dangereuses*.[11] In London, areas like Hackney and Tottenham

9   See, e.g., Sunita Menon, "Captive Workers Escape from Housing Compound," *Gulf News*, March 7, 2005.

10   A quote from the Catholic conservative writer Louis Veuillot, cited in Eric Hazan, *The Invention of Paris: A History in Footsteps* (London: Verso, 2011 [2002]), 131.

11   A phrase coined by the French civil servant H. A. Frégier just a few years before Haussmann's renovation of Paris began that captures the bourgeois idea about the urban poor as threatening criminals. See Marie Marmo Mullaney, "Frégier and the 'Dangerous Classes': Poverty in Orleanist France," *International Social Science Review* 58.2 (1983), 88–92. On contemporary versions of Haussmann, see Neil Smith, *The New*

that saw unrest in the riots that took place during the summer of 2011 were identified for larger scale gentification and redevelopment. Many American cities engaged in urban renewal in response to riots and their perceived threat to social order. The repressive geographies of Parisian *banlieues* facilitate surveillance by the police, even as they feed a sense of grievance that inspires conflict in the first place.[12] In Istanbul, redevelopment around Taksim Square and Tarlabaşşı seems intended to pacify areas seen as disorderly and noncompliant. In cities across Latin America, informal neighborhoods were long seen as hotbeds of insurrection that therefore needed to be bulldozed.

In more extreme cases, housing has been directly targeted for collective punishment or military conquest. "Domicide," or the intentional destruction of homes, is a way to assert sovereignty over territory or to erase a competing group's claim to place.[13]

Urban Frontier: Gentrification and the Revanchist City (London: Routledge, 1996); Loretta Lees, Hyun Bang Shin, and Ernesto López-Morales, eds, *Global Gentrifications: Uneven Development and Displacement* (Bristol: Policy Press, 2015); and cf. Andy Merrifield's discussion of "neo-Haussmannization" in *The New Urban Question* (London: Pluto Press, 2014). For a discussion of how contemporary urban renewal in the United States differs from its mid-century predecessor, see Derek S. Hyra, "Conceptualizing the New Urban Renewal: Comparing the Past to the Present," *Urban Affairs Review* 48.4 (2012), 498–527.

12   On "repressive geographies" of the *banlieues*, see Mustafa Dikeç, *Badlands of the Republic: Space, Politics, and Urban Policy* (Malden, MA: Blackwell, 2007), 158–62.

13   J. Douglas Porteous and Sandra E. Smith, *Domicide: The Global Destruction of Home* (Montreal: McGill-Queens University Press, 2001); Mel Nowicki, "Rethinking Domicide: Towards an Expanded Critical Geography of Home," *Geography Compass* 8.11 (2014), 785–95.

The "deliberate killing of home" was used throughout the history of European colonialism and remains a global problem.[14] Recent examples include the 1990s conflict in Bosnia, which was, in part, a war of "homelands against homes" where the annihilation of "dwelling the Bosnian way" was pursued as a military objective.[15] And since 1967, the Israeli Defense Forces have been demolishing Palestinian homes in the West Bank and the Gaza Strip, a situation that Amnesty International and other human rights groups have identified as "collective punishment."[16] According to the United Nations, in one section of the West Bank alone, between 1988 and 2014, more than 14,000 Palestinian homes were destroyed following demolition orders issued by the Israeli Civil Administration.[17]

The deliberate demolition of homes is brutal. But it would be a mistake to suppose that residential oppression only appears in times of warfare or civil unrest. Oppression should be seen, instead, as a terrible but routine part of the housing systems of many countries of the world today.

---

14   Porteous and Smith, *Domicide*, 12.

15   Gearóid Ó Tuathail and Carl Dahlman, "Post-domicide Bosnia and Herzegovina: Homes, Homelands and One Million Returns," *International Peacekeeping* 13.2 (2006), 242–60.

16   Amnesty International, *Families under the Rubble: Israeli Attacks on Inhabited Homes* (London: Amnesty International, 2014); B'Tselem, "House Demolition as Punishment," November 26, 2014; Christopher Harker, "Spacing Palestine through the Home," *Transactions of the Institute of British Geographers* 34.3 (2009), 320–32; Amnesty International, "Israel/Occupied Territories: House Demolition," September 29, 2005.

17   United Nations Office for the Coordination of Humanitarian Affairs, *Under Threat: Demolition Orders in Area C of the West Bank* (East Jerusalem: UNOCHA, 2015), 5.

The repressive dimension to displacement has not received as much attention as other issues in debates about gentrification, but it is significant. Expensive real estate may fail to meet most people's needs for a place to live, but for city governments looking to quell dissent and attract global capital, it is both economically and politically advantageous. A city where the dangerous classes have been removed does not rebel. The more householders are required to work and struggle to keep up, the more are they focused on merely surviving and avoiding the negative sanctions that might lead to their removal.

The hyper-commodified city is bound to be an oppressive city. Housing that is not home but simply money in dwelling form requires no services, makes no demands, poses no challenge to the ruling order. The zones of empty luxury housing in the centers of global cities are as peaceful as cemeteries. Commodification is not only a strategy for capital accumulation. It is also a technique of governance, a political process as much as an economic one.

Oppression and Ownership

Oppressive uses of housing need not be violent. In some cases, residential oppression can be quite pleasant for those affected, at least in the short term. Just as prison can be a punishment for insurrection, good housing can be used as a reward for obedience. The promise of higher-quality housing, for example, was a way to secure political acquiescence from Party members in the Soviet Union.[18] Similarly, the distribution of information

---

18   Henry W. Morton, "Who Gets What, When and How? Housing in the Soviet Union," *Soviet Studies* 32.2 (1980), 235–59.

and contacts about housing was an integral part of machine politics in many American cities. In unequal systems, privilege is the flip side of privation, and the threat of the latter is a way to maintain the loyalty of those who enjoy the former.

No form of tenure enjoys greater privileges today than private ownership. It is ultimately the political dimension of homeownership that explains its prominent place in American ideology. As much as there are economic reasons for its dominance, the cultish devotion to ownership suggests that it also plays a wider political role.[19]

The political functionality of homeownership has been apparent to authorities for a long time. Weighing the question of how to organize land tenure in colonial North America, the Privy Council of England declared, in 1772, "Experience shows that the possession of property is the best security for a due obedience and submission to government."[20] Property qualification for

---

19   Peter Marcuse, "A Critical Approach to the Subprime Mortgage Crisis in the United States: Rethinking the Public Sector in Housing," *City and Community* 8.3 (2009), 351–6; Lynne Dearborn, "Homeownership: The Problematics of Ideals and Realities," *Journal of Affordable Housing and Community Development Law* 16.1 (2006), 40–51; Richard Harris and Chris Hamnett, "The Myth of the Promised Land: The Social Diffusion of Home Ownership in Britain and North America," *Annals of the Association of American Geographers* 77.2 (1987), 173–90; Jim Kemeny, *The Myth of Home Ownership: Private versus Public Choices in Housing Tenure* (London: Routledge and Kegan Paul, 1981); Matthew Edel, Elliott D. Sclar, and Daniel Luria, *Shaky Palaces: Homeownership and Social Mobility in Boston's Suburbanization* (New York: Columbia University Press, 1986).

20   Quoted in Andro Linklater, *Owning the Earth: The Transforming History of Land Ownership* (London: Bloomsbury, 2013), 235.

voting has feudal antecedents, but it was long maintained as an integral part of democracy, and it underpinned the disenfranchisement of the propertyless in the early United States. It was useful for separating the dangerous rabble from democratic subjects, who were held to be proper citizens because they were property owners. It ensured that those citizens empowered to vote would never risk upsetting the stability of the system.

In the twentieth century, homeownership was seen not only as crucial ideological medicine to maintain the beating heart of consumerism, but also as inoculation against radical alternatives. The housing economist Homer Hoyt put the matter bluntly in 1966: "Communism can never win in a nation of homeowners."[21] The political aspect of homeownership was central to Margaret Thatcher's invocation of a "property-owning democracy" and George W. Bush's similar image of an "ownership society." And the sense that homeownership is the key to personal prosperity and social stability is prominent in the housing policies of Barack Obama as well as David Cameron, who explicitly harkens back to Thatcher's veneration of property ownership—despite the manifest failures of homeownership to ease residential problems in the past decade.

The reign of private ownership serves the interests of dominant classes and groups in many ways.[22] Homeownership increases both the economic profitability and the political stability of the system. It inhibits the potential for opposition by holding out the

---

21   Homer Hoyt, *According to Hoyt: Fifty Years of Homer Hoyt* (Washington, DC: Homer Hoyt Associates, 1966), 156.

22   Which is one reason why Engels's chief antagonists in *The Housing Question* were bourgeois reformers who believed they could solve the housing question through private homeownership.

possibility of a "stake in the system."[23] Particularly in countries like the United States, Canada, the United Kingdom, or Australia, where rates of homeownership are high, its stabilizing role can hardly be exaggerated. During both the Great Depression and the 2008 mortgage crisis, widespread residential suffering did not suffice to move the United States government to action; but when the situations threatened to turn into broader crises of the legitimacy of the state, swift ameliorative action was taken. In stabilizing the social and political order, however, homeownership also conserves a housing system that is in fact intolerable for many.

Owning a home has provided economic security for some. For the affluent, paying off a mortgage during their working years is a form of saving for old age. But for plenty of working- and middle-class households, the commitment to homeownership as the only feasible way of obtaining decent housing is oppressive. The constant burden of mortgage payments is an economic hardship, forcing them to allocate far more of their income to housing than they would wish, to work overtime, or to take additional jobs.

The economic burdens of homeownership have political consequences. Iris Marion Young argued, "The goal of a dream house sets workers working and keeps workers working, fearing job loss, working overtime. The consumer-driven desire of civic privatism tends to produce political quietism."[24] Ownership

---

23 Kemeny, *The Myth of Home Ownership*; Matthew Edel, "Home Ownership and Working Class Unity," *International Journal of Urban and Regional Research* 6.2 (1982), 205–22; Peter Saunders, "Domestic Property and Social Class," *International Journal of Urban and Regional Research* 2.1–4 (1978), 233–51.

24 Iris Marion Young, *Intersecting Voices: Dilemmas of Gender, Political Philosophy, and Policy* (Princeton, NJ: Princeton University Press, 1997), 143.

restricts household members' opportunities to engage in other activities, as well as their desires to do so, especially their willingness to participate in collective action that might involve social conflict. And the privatization and individualization of housing leads to the internalization of problems. If something goes wrong, the individual is thought to be to blame rather than social and political structures.

The hegemony of homeownership is system-conserving in other ways as well. Homeownership can be used to present the interests of individual households as aligned with the interests of the real estate industry. It facilitates political manipulation through the threat of falling property values. It reduces the demand for state action, as rising house prices are seen as compensation for insufficient social services. Above all, it gives homeowners an economic stake in maintaining scarcity and sustaining the housing crisis—and in supporting political parties that will do what they can to keep prices high. In unstable times, ownership remains the best tool for generating support for an unequal system.

The Intersectionality of Residential Oppression

The use of housing to maintain the status quo is widespread, but residential oppression is not experienced uniformly. The housing system intersects with stratification and exclusion in complicated ways.[25] Poor households are oppressed more than

---

25 The general concept of intersectionality refers to what Leslie McCall calls "the relationships among multiple dimensions and modalities of social relations and subject formations," i.e., the ways in which multiple social categories interact and create distinctive experiences of oppression, with a particular focus on the

others, an experience which cuts across other social divisions and identities. But in addition to the effects of income, particular groups face distinct forms of residential oppression.

As feminists have long demonstrated, housing and patriarchy are intimately connected. Due to the gendered division of labor, the household should be seen as a site of struggle.[26] Historically, gender conflict within the home was rooted in "two characteristics of industrial capitalism: the physical separation of household space from public space, and the economic separation of the domestic economy from the political economy."[27] Women were confined to exploitative toil within the home. Due to the "labor of women in the house," Charlotte Perkins Gilman wrote in 1898, "women are economic factors in society," yet "whatever the economic value of the domestic industry of women is, they do not get it."[28] The spatial separation between workplace

---

intersections of patriarchy and racism. We invoke the concept here to signal the ways that housing oppression intersects with other categories. See Leslie McCall, "The Complexity of Intersectionality," *Signs: Journal of Women in Culture and Society* 30.3 (2005), 1771–1800; Kimberle Crenshaw, "Mapping the Margins: Intersectionality, Identity Politics, and Violence against Women of Color," *Stanford Law Review* 43.6 (1991), 1241–99.

26   See Heidi I. Hartmann, "The Family as the Locus of Gender, Class, and Political Struggle: The Example of Housework," *Signs* 6.3 (1981), 366–94.

27   Dolores Hayden, *The Grand Domestic Revolution: A History of Feminist Designs for American Homes, Neighborhoods, and Cities* (Cambridge, MA: MIT Press, 1981), 1.

28   Charlotte Perkins Gilman, *Women and Economics: A Study of the Economic Relation between Men and Women as a Factor in Social Evolution* (Berkeley: University of California Press, 1998 [1898]), 13, 14.

and home, and the privatization of domestic labor within separate housing units, bolstered this form of gender oppression.

Today female participation in the waged workforce is higher than ever. But plenty of women still perform a second shift of domestic work. And beyond the issue of household labor, there are many ways that housing can facilitate women's oppression. For example, women can be subjected to sexual harassment and assault by their landlords, a form of oppression that is not as widely discussed as sexual harassment in the workplace but which is in fact a terrorizing invasion of domestic space.[29] Female-headed households may contend with discrimination, and they can be stigmatized as undesirable "problem families."[30] Of course not all women are subjected to the same forms of residential oppression. Queer and transgender women, disabled women, female seniors, and women of color all confront distinct forms of exclusion and subjugation in housing.

Housing is also implicated in systemic racism. For communities of color, housing can become an instrument for the denial of basic elements of modern democratic citizenship that others take for granted, such as decent education facilities, employment, transportation access, and fair treatment by police and the courts.

---

29   Griff Tester, "An Intersectional Analysis of Sexual Harassment in Housing," *Gender and Society* 22.3 (2008), 349–66; Maggie E. Reed, Linda L. Collinsworth, and Louise F. Fitzgerald, "There's No Place Like Home: Sexual Harassment of Low Income Women in Housing," *Psychology, Public Policy and Law* 11.3 (2005), 439–62.

30   Imogen Tyler, "Chav Mum Chav Scum: Class Disgust in Contemporary Britain," *Feminist Media Studies* 8.1 (2008), 17–34; Paul Michael Garrett, "'Sinbin' Solutions: The 'Pioneer' Projects for 'Problem Families' and the Forgetfulness of Social Policy Research," *Critical Social Policy* 27.2 (2007), 203–30.

In the United States, property has always been intertwined with race. Anti-black racism and white supremacy were foundational to the housing system. Residential control and separation have been used to exploit black people's labor, to divide their resources, and to undercut their political power. This pattern can be seen in housing conditions in both the North and the South before the Civil War, in Jim Crow policies, in de jure and de facto residential segregation, in redlining, in urban renewal—as well as in the predatory lending, unequal rates of incarceration, and violent policing of African-Americans' housing all of which are still apparent in today's cities. Many white Americans may prefer to see this story as ancient history. But communities of color continue to encounter distinct forms of housing oppression.[31] Racial segregation continues to be a major problem throughout the country.[32] And both African-Americans and

---

31   See Elvin Wyly, C. S. Ponder, Pierson Nettling, Bosco Ho, Sophie Ellen Fung, Zachary Liebowitz, and Dan Hammel, "New Racial Meanings of Housing in America," *American Quarterly* 64.3 (2012), 571–604.

32   Samantha Friedman, Hui-shien Tsao, and Cheng Chen, "Housing Tenure and Residential Segregation in Metropolitan America," *Demography* 50.4 (2013), 1477–98; Steven R. Holloway, Richard Wright, and Mark Ellis, "The Racially Fragmented City? Neighborhood Racial Segregation and Diversity Jointly Considered," *Professional Geographer* 64.1 (2012), 63–82; Ron Johnston, Michael Poulsen, and James Forrest, "And Did the Walls Come Tumbling Down? Ethnic Residential Segregation in Four U.S. Metropolitan Areas 1980–2000," *Urban Geography* 24.7 (2003), 560–81; Camille Zubrinsky Charles, "The Dynamics of Racial Residential Segregation," *Annual Review of Sociology* 29 (2003), 167–207; Lincoln Quillian, "Why Is Black–White Residential Segregation So Persistent? Evidence on Three Theories from Migration Data," *Social Science Research* 31.2 (2002), 197–229.

Latino/as continue to be charged a racist premium for housing, both as renters and as homeowners.[33]

The normative ideal of the home as a space of freedom and protection obscures racist inequalities in residential sanctity. Ofelia O. Cuevas observes that in the United States, the homes of black and brown people "have never provided the presumed guarantee against state or extralegal violence that the home is understood to provide for whites." Ontological security is a privilege denied to households of color. Their dwellings were never treated as inviolable sanctuaries. "We should thus not be surprised by the routine violence with which the homes of black and brown people are subjected to by police, frequently with fatal consequences."[34] One of the most tragic recent examples took place in Detroit on May 16, 2010. Using a flash grenade, police searching for a suspect burst into the house of an African-American family, and in the process shot and killed seven-year-old Aiyana Stanley-Jones while she was sleeping on the couch. In general, the

33   Keith Ihlanfeldt and Tom Mayock, "Price Discrimination in the Housing Market," *Journal of Urban Economics* 66.2 (2009), 125–40; Elvin K. Wyly and Daniel J. Hammel, "Gentrification, Segregation, and Discrimination in the American Urban System," *Environment and Planning A* 36 (2004), 1215–41; Caitlin Knowles Myers, "Discrimination and Neighborhood Effects: Understanding Racial Differentials in US Housing Prices," *Journal of Urban Economics* 56.2 (2004), 279–302; David R. Harris, "'Property Values Drop When Blacks Move in, Because . . .': Racial and Socioeconomic Determinants of Neighborhood Desirability," *American Sociological Review* 64.3 (1999), 461–79.

34   Ofelia O. Cuevas, "Welcome to My Cell: Housing and Race in the Mirror of American Democracy," *American Quarterly* 64.3 (2012), 610.

homes of people of color are the primary targets of searches that use paramilitary force.[35]

Race and gender are obviously not the only social categories that intersect with residential repression and exploitation. A study of the residential experiences of mothers of Caribbean and African origin who are HIV-positive living in Toronto, for example, illustrates just how complex the overlapping sources of exclusion and oppression can be. These women confront "Eurocentric housing, health and social care systems that did not address their needs as racialized and ethnic minorities. This included housing policies that failed to consider how culture, language issues and experiences of social isolation and HIV-related stigma" shaped their housing access.[36] Households navigate complex fields of hierarchy and oppression. Citizenship status, disability, language, and other forms of social differentiation all interact with the housing system in different ways.

As varied as these distinct forms of residential oppression might seem, their patterns are not random. They come about because the housing system is embedded in social structures, and they reflect the lines of antagonism and power in class society.

If the geometries of residential oppression and other social categories are complex, the question of who benefits from this oppression seems deceptively simple: the "oppressors," of

---

35   American Civil Liberties Union, *War Comes Home: The Excessive Militarization of American Policing* (New York: ACLU, 2014) 35–6.

36   Saara Greene, Lori Chambers, Khatundi Masinde, and Doris O'Brien-Teengs, "A House Is Not a Home: The Housing Experiences of African and Caribbean Mothers Living with HIV," *Housing Studies* 28.1 (2013), 121.

course. But again there is no single category. Benefits from residential oppression appear as payments, fees, votes, influence, entitlements, privileges, consent, and a thousand other forms. In some instances—for example, a landlord charging higher rent to a tenant with undocumented immigration status—the relation between oppression and profit is unmistakable. In others, such as the micro-aggressions directed at public housing tenants, the question of who benefits may be less certain, though the harm is real nonetheless.

Liberation, or Resistance to Oppression

Can housing also serve as a tool for resisting residential oppression? Can it be an instrument for liberation? Traditionally, in both liberal and radical social thought, it was not housing but the workplace that was seen as the proper site to counter oppression.[37] Engels was only the most prominent voice to warn against seeking an "isolated solution of the housing question."[38] Residential struggles, as conflicts involving consumption rather than production, were typically treated as secondary issues. The theoretical argument is that consumption-oriented conflicts can at best produce minor and reformist victories and at worst misdirect energies that should go into "proper" arenas of struggle. Only to the extent that movements around housing are linked to workplace politics, goes the argument, can they have real significance.

---

37   See Jeff Weintraub and Krishan Kumar, eds, *Public and Private in Thought and Practice: Perspectives on a Grand Dichotomy* (Chicago: The University of Chicago Press, 1997).

38   Frederick [*sic*] Engels, *The Housing Question*, ed. C. P. Dutt (London: Laurence and Wishart, 1936 [1872]) 73.

The traditional privileging of industrial over residential politics, however, provides a limited basis for understanding housing, much less changing it. It is part of a way of conceiving of politics that sidelines "private" struggles within the home and effectively normalizes the subjugation of women.[39] It misunderstands housing as merely a site of consumption, not one of production and social reproduction. It ignores the growing significance of real estate in the current global system. And it offers an impoverished vision of political resistance. People resist in as many ways as they are oppressed. Whether one can better deal with oppressive conditions through activities "in production" or in the neighborhood, at work or at home, or in some other site using some other political language, is ultimately a practical question, not something to be predetermined in the abstract.[40]

The idea that housing has emancipatory potential is derived from concrete experience. Housing patterns are not imposed by all-powerful forces on passive and helpless victims. Residents find ways to resist. It is clear that residential struggles will not, on their own, lead to wholesale social transformation. But movements across the world show that housing can be a critical resource for resistance to oppression.

---

39   See virtually any feminist writing on the public/private distinction, e.g., Carol Pateman, "Feminist Critiques of the Public/ Private Dichotomy," pp. 281–303 in S. I. Benn and G. F. Gaus, *Public and Private in Social Life* (New York: St. Martin's Press, 1983).

40   The political and social consequences of the division between work and home are addressed in depth in Ira Katznelson's classic *City Trenches: Urban Politics and the Patterning of Class in the United States* (Chicago: The University of Chicago Press, 1981).

The clearest examples of residents using their dwellings in acts of resistance come from struggles that directly concern housing itself. It is true that there are some residential conflicts that are restricted to purely economic matters, in the narrow sense of bargaining between supplier and user of housing as to the payment to be made for it. But in many, if not most, cases transactional bargaining cannot be disentangled from political claims about justice, rights, and power.

The rent strike is the classic form of resistance to oppression in housing.[41] The tactic's most famous example began in Glasgow in April 1915, a high point of the period of insurgency known as Red Clydeside. An acute housing shortage led to spiraling rents, overcrowding, and dilapidation. Housing need was exacerbated by a growing concentration of industrial laborers recruited to the shipbuilding and munitions industries, an opportunity which local landlords did not fail to seize.[42] By November of that year, 20,000 households were on strike. Organized by tenant committees, women's associations, labor organizations, and leftist parties, the strike saw residential battles waged in the streets, in the courts, and in Parliament. Fearing the spread of insurrection to the factories, the state responded

---

41   See Joseph Melling, "The Glasgow Rent Strike and Clydeside Labour: Some Problems of Interpretation," *Scottish Labour History Society Journal* 13 (1979), 39–44; Manuel Castells, *The City and the Grassroots: A Cross-cultural Theory of Urban Social Movements* (Berkeley: University of California Press, 1983), 27–37.

42   Castells, *The City and the Grassroots*, 28, notes that in 1911, just a few years before the strike, "in the midst of the urban crisis, 11 per cent of Glasgow's housing stock was vacant for reasons of speculation." Furthermore, "landlords and rentiers obtained more benefit by overcrowding existing habitations . . . than by building new housing with longer and uncertain rates of return."

with eviction freezes and rent controls, and contributed to the rise of public housing in Scotland and throughout the United Kingdom.

In the Glasgow rent strikes, residential and industrial issues were interlaced. As much as the strikes were centered on issues of collective consumption and in fact supported by various industrialists, Manuel Castells argues, "the Rent Strike provided a broad common ground for the unity of the different segments of the working class at the community level."[43] Resisting their landlords was one of the ways in which working-class Glaswegians contested the existing order.

In their more contentious manifestations, rent strikes are about more than just rent. Early twentieth-century rent strikes in New York, Chicago, Buenos Aires, Santiago, and elsewhere drew on radical currents from socialist, communist, and anarchist movements.[44] The combative rent strikes in the East End of London in the late 1930s were "part of a wider battle for Communism" and against fascism in what was then a heavily Jewish neighborhood.[45]

Other residential uprisings are about autonomy, control, and the politics of racial and ethnic exclusion. In the massive rent strike in public housing in St. Louis beginning in 1969, the issue was not only or even predominantly about how much rent should

---

43 Ibid., 31.

44 For a comparative analysis, see Andrew Wood and James A. Baer, "Strength in Numbers: Urban Rent Strikes and Political Transformation in the Americas, 1904–1925," *Journal of Urban History* 32.6 (2006), 862–84.

45 Sarah Glynn, "East End Immigrants and the Battle for Housing: A Comparative Study of Political Mobilisation in the Jewish and Bengali Communities," *Journal of Historical Geography* 31.3 (2005), 529.

be paid: it was about who was in charge and who was responsible for residential conditions. The strikers evinced what one observer called a "new sense of self-determination" aligned with the "social revolution" of the Black Power movement.[46] Rhonda Williams details how in Baltimore in the 1970s "tenant power" became a widespread slogan "echoing the call for black power and reflecting poor people's contemporary grassroots fights for rights and voice."[47] Another wave of rent strikes in London's East End in the 1970s was part of Bengali antiracist politics and black radicalism in Britain. From 1975 until 1980, tens of thousands of migrant workers of African origin conducted a long rent strike against the semi-public hostels in which they were housed in various locations in the Paris region, a major moment in the history of migrant rights and antiracist activism in France.[48]

Across the globe, rent strikes have been tools in anticolonial struggles. In the Irish Land War of the late nineteenth century, rent strikes were mounted across Ireland as part of the movement for home rule. A rent strike in Zanzibar in the 1920s "can be considered one of the first tangible steps" towards independence achieved four decades later.[49] Rent strikes were used across

---

46   Michael Karp, "The St. Louis Rent Strike of 1969: Transforming Black Activism and American Low-Income Housing," *Journal of Urban History* 40.4 (2014), 657.

47   Rhonda Y. Williams, *The Politics of Public Housing: Black Women's Struggles against Urban Inequality* (New York: Oxford University Press, 2004), 176.

48   See Jean-Philippe Dedieu and Aissatou Mbodj-Pouye, "The First Collective Protest of Black African Migrants in Postcolonial France (1960–1975): A Struggle for Housing and Rights," forthcoming in *Ethnic and Racial Studies*.

49   Garth Andrew Myers, "Sticks and Stones: Colonialism and Zanzibari Housing," *Africa* 67.2 (1997), 260.

India in the movement against British control. Waves of rent strikes in South African townships in the late 1980s contributed to the downfall of apartheid.

In all of these examples, tenants were organizing, often at great personal and collective risk, against oppressive residential conditions. But at the same time they were part of bigger political movements.

The other major way in which residents have directly fought housing oppression is through anti-eviction direct action and its close relative, anti-foreclosure activism. The prevention and reversal of evictions have roots in the earliest struggles over land tenure. In the modern era, in response to the commodification of housing under industrial capitalism, residents formed anti-eviction committees, organized squats, broke locks, blocked marshals, guarded furniture that had been thrown onto the street, and moved evicted families back into their apartments.

Today, anti-eviction and anti-foreclosure activism takes a huge variety of forms. Chicago's Anti-eviction Campaign fights to prevent residents from being removed from their homes and breaks into abandoned properties in order to place "home-less people into the people-less homes."[50] In addition to organizing mortgage strikes, a Cleveland-based group called ESOP throws two-inch plastic sharks at the homes of bankers while distributing flyers announcing, "Your neighbor is a loan shark."[51] In South

---

50   Ben Austen, "The Death and Life of Chicago," *New York Times*, May 29, 2013.

51   David Bornstein, "Foreclosure Is Not an Option," *New York Times*, December 6, 2010. ESOP originally stood for East Side Organizing Project; now it means Empowering and Strengthening Ohio's People. See also Michael McQuarrie, "ESOP Rises Again," *Shelterforce*, September 2, 2010.

Africa, the Western Cape Anti-Eviction Campaign uses direct action and legal challenges against evictions and water cutoffs. In the UK, the East London–based group Focus E15 Mothers organizes eviction watches and demonstrations, and occupied an empty public housing complex in protest.[52] The Plataforma de Afectados por la Hipoteca (Platform for People Affected by Mortgages), founded in Barcelona and active across Spain, fights against evictions and foreclosures using tactics borrowed both from the struggle against military dictatorship in Argentina and from the Spanish Indignados movement of which they are a part.

For these groups, the eviction question is one part of larger struggles. Take Back the Land is a Miami-based group that has blocked evictions, moved homeless families into foreclosed homes, and founded Umoja Village, a shantytown on empty land, as a way to draw attention to the connections between land, gentrification, and homelessness. Max Rameau, one of the group's founders, wrote, "The housing crisis . . . is not in and of itself the problem. Rather, the housing crisis is a glaring symptom of a larger, deeper problem rooted in class, race and gender. Those are the Systemic Issues."[53]

These examples show that contesting residential oppression is a way to fight for political and social change more broadly. Far from proposing isolated solutions to the housing problem, they aim at politicizing housing and excavating its relationships to deeper social crises.

It is the case that these movements have been more successful when they have linked up with mobilizations in other

---

52 Focus E15 is the name of a hostel from which the original members of the group, composed of single mothers, were evicted.

53 Max Rameau, *Take Back the Land: Land, Gentrification and the Umoja Village Shantytown* (Oakland, CA: AK Press, 2012), 41.

sectors. And not all of them have led to enduring political organization. Some, drawing on exclusionary ethnic identities, have taken reactionary turns or undercut more radical political projects. But taken as a whole they demonstrate that activists see housing campaigns as being about more than just housing. For their participants, rent strikes, anti-eviction rallies, and anti-foreclosure marches have broader transformative potential.

Prefiguring Liberation

Housing is not only the object of struggle. In some cases it offers a glimpse of what non-alienated social life might look like.

Home can be a source of autonomy and strength. The critic and activist bell hooks captures this side of housing:

> Historically, African-American people believed that the construction of a homeplace, however fragile and tenuous (the slave hut, the wooden shack), had a radical political dimension. Despite the brutal reality of racial apartheid, of domination, one's homeplace was the one site where one could freely confront the issue of humanization, where one could resist.[54]

For hooks, the homeplace is "where all black people could strive to be subjects, not objects, where we could be affirmed in our minds and hearts despite poverty, hardship, and deprivation."[55]

---

54 bell hooks, *Yearning: Race, Gender, and Cultural Politics* (New York: Routledge, 2015 [1990]), 42.

55 Ibid.

In the face of alienation and oppression, home at least offers the possibility of agency and solidarity.

Housing movements worldwide pursue strategies centered on disalienation, dignity, citizenship, and care. Activists in New York, London, and elsewhere are exploring practices of "militant care" by engaging in direct-action mutual aid.[56] São Paulo's União de Movimentos de Moradia (Alliance of Housing Movements—UMM) aims to make it possible for everyone who is *sem teto*—without a roof—to "feel like a person." A woman who moved into a building that had been occupied by a UMM affiliate told a researcher, "Today I feel much more of a citizen than I did before. When I came to live here, I 'rescued' a bit more of my citizenship."[57] Similarly, the South African movement Abahlali baseMjondolo (Shack Dwellers), founded in Durban, has held marches to "Defend Dignity and Demand

---

56   Examples of militant care in action would be the grassroots disaster response in New York known as Occupy Sandy; self-organized responses to flooding in 2014 in Serbia and Bosnia and Herzegovina; and the grassroots aid offered to refugees and migrants in Calais. See "Militant Care," issue 28 of the *Occupied Times of London*, especially Manuela Zechner and Bue Rübner Hansen, "Social Reproduction and Collective Care: A Horizon for Struggles and Practices," *Occupied Times* 28 (2015), 6–7. See also Tom Gann, "A Path through the Embers: A Militant Caring Infrastructure against Revanchist South London," in his blog *A Handbook for City Renters*, May 11, 2015, which draws in part on his work with the group Housing Action Southwark & Lambeth. Cf. Peter Marcuse, "Spatial Justice: Derivative but Causal of Social Justice," *Justice Spatiale/Spatial Justice* 1 (2009), 2.

57   Lucy Earle, "From Insurgent to Transgressive Citizenship: Housing, Social Movements and the Politics of Rights in São Paulo," *Journal of Latin American Studies* 44 (2012), 117–18.

Land & Housing." In February 2015, the group presented a statement to the Human Rights Commission in Johannesburg where they elucidated the residential politics of dignity:

> By dignity we mean respect. When we say that we are struggling for dignity we mean that we are struggling for a society in which each person is recognised as a human being. This means that they must be treated with respect but also that they must have access to all that a person needs for a dignified life—land, housing, education, a livelihood and so on.[58]

In a world where the dignity of working-class and poor people is under attack and where poor people's housing is so often a source of alienation, the idea of universal access to home as a place of dignity has radical potential.

Feminist work on housing shows what a non-oppressive residential environment might look like. Generations of feminists envisioned emancipation from drudgery through technology and the reorganization of domestic labor; the end of unequal work burdens; the breaking down of the restraints of the traditional bourgeois household; the creation of common spaces to support labor sharing and enjoyable social interaction; and the development of new forms of liberation. In the nineteenth and early twentieth centuries, American feminists like Victoria

---

58 Reprinted as Abahlali baseMjondolo, "Statement to the Human Rights Commission," *Occupied Times*, March 9, 2015. See South African Human Rights Commission, "The South African Human Rights Commission Investigative Hearing Report: Access to Housing, Local Governance and Service Delivery," February 23–5, 2015.

Woodhull, Charlotte Perkins Gilman, and Melusina Fay Pierce proposed cooperative kitchens, wages for housework, socialized childcare, and other ways of politicizing and collectivizing the domestic workplace. Alexandra Kollontai promoted similar ideas in the Soviet Union.[59]

For centuries, architects and utopians have pursued the idea that housing can provide the basis for a humane society. Such projects return again and again to the same themes: decommodification, collective amenities, social spaces, democratic self-management, and engagement with the political and cultural life of residents. Many proposals along these lines appeared only as unbuilt plans or incomplete prototypes, like Charles Fourier's nineteenth-century *phalanstère* or Moscow's Narkomfin Building, designed by Moisei Ginzburg in 1928. But some were built and served as actually existing experiments in emancipatory dwelling.[60]

The great housing estates of Red Vienna are among the best examples of an emancipatory residential environment. The city council, controlled by the Social Democrats from 1919, built tens of thousands of apartments as dense perimeter blocks of housing and communal amenities constructed around courtyards (*Höfe*). Ultimately the city built more than 60,000 apartments in ten years. They were named after revolutionary and cultural figures: Bebelhof, Goethehof, Friedrich Engels Platz, George Washington Hof. The most famous, Karl Marx Hof,

---

59   See Dolores Hayden, *The Grand Domestic Revolution: A History of Feminist Designs for American Homes, Neighborhoods, and Cities* (Cambridge, MA: MIT Press, 1981).

60   For a discussion of how "socialist architects have often created glimpses of what a different society could look like," see Owen Hatherley, "Imagining the Socialist City," *Jacobin* 15–16 (2014), 95–101.

constructed between 1927 and 1930, was seen both by its residents and by their enemies as a fortress of municipal socialism. The developments formed the physical as well as social structure around which the Viennese working class conducted its activities, held itself together, identified itself. During the crisis of February 1934, federal troops attacked the buildings as symbols of social democracy. But they survived as central parts of the Viennese urban fabric and remain so to this day.[61]

Cooperative housing developments in New York City were the contemporaneous American counterparts to the social-democratic housing of Vienna. These buildings were a direct outgrowth of the labor movement and the radical culture that had grown up with it in New York's working-class, immigrant neighborhoods. The city's first nonprofit cooperative was built starting in 1916 in Sunset Park, Brooklyn. Created by the Finnish Home Building Association and named Alku ("Beginning" in Finnish), the building drew on Scandinavian traditions of cooperative housing. And from the 1920s through the 1970s, largely Jewish labor unions and cooperative associations built or financed 40,000 housing units in the city. Concentrated in the Lower East Side and especially in the Bronx, these nonprofit, limited-equity complexes include the United Workers Cooperative Colony, the Amalgamated

---

61 Stadt Wien, "Municipal Housing in Vienna: History, Facts and Figures" (2013); Peter Marcuse, "A Useful Installment of Socialist Work: Housing in Red Vienna," pp. 558–85 in Bratt, Hartman, and Meyerson, *Critical Perspectives on Housing*. While much of the housing of Red Vienna still stands, like decommodified housing across the world, it is under threat of redevelopment. See Justin Kadi, "Recommodifying Housing in Formerly 'Red' Vienna?," *Housing, Theory and Society* 32.3 (2015), 247–65.

Housing Cooperative, Amalgamated Dwellings, Shalom Aleichem Houses, Hillman Housing, and the Farband Houses. Aligned with political movements ranging from Labor Zionism to Der Arbeter Ring to Leninism, these projects were, according to a former resident of one of the radical Bronx cooperatives, "a little corner of socialism right in New York."[62]

The Bronx co-op buildings themselves tended towards a conservative Tudor revival style. But labor historian Joshua Freeman remarks, "The architecturally conventional outer skins of these projects masked bold experiments in the creation of self-contained political communities, rich in educational, social, and cultural activities."[63] They included a range of social spaces, such as libraries, cinemas, lecture halls, health clinics, restaurants, cooperative shops, performance spaces, and meeting rooms. For the co-ops' residents, "activism was a way of life."[64] They formed the backbone of the tenacious 1932 rent strike that took place nearby, and participated in many other campaigns and movements.

Today monuments to alternative dwelling like Karl Marx Hof or the Bronx co-ops might seem like artifacts from another civilization. But many of their ideas have filtered into the contemporary housing system. Gated communities carry echoes of the experimental utopian enclave. Luxury apartment towers

---

62   Mark Naison, "From Eviction Resistance to Rent Control: Tenant Activism in the Great Depression," pp. 94–133 in Ronald Lawson with Mark Naison, eds, *The Tenant Movement in New York City, 1904–1984* (New Brunswick, NJ: Rutgers University Press, 1986), 103.

63   Joshua B. Freeman, "Red New York," *Monthly Review* 54.3 (2002), 38.

64   Naison, "From Eviction Resistance to Rent Control," 103.

provide shared spaces for consumption. Elements of radical housing experiments persist today, but often in privatized and commodified form.

There are good reasons to be skeptical of utopian housing experiments. Human relationships cannot be confined to the boundaries of a housing estate. It is not possible to insulate a small group from what goes on in society as a whole; any such group is likely to be shaped by broader patterns of oppressive relationships. And islands of residential liberation will have limited impact in a sea of housing oppression and commodification.

But experimental dwellings and emancipatory movements have wider significance as living demonstrations of housing's potential. They should be seen as beacons pointing towards a broader possibility: that housing might support non-oppressive social relations, not in some utopian realm but in everyday life.

Residential liberation has a much deeper content than simply making housing more affordable or accessible. Affordable housing is not a challenge to the ruling class. It can be provided in the name of social stability, as New Dealers like Langdon Post understood. The challenge today is to imagine a housing system that enables residents to confront power, social inequality, and structural violence in a more significant way.

For a Repoliticized Housing Debate

Housing is always more than just housing. But contemporary debates do not reckon with residential oppression and emancipation. Housing needs to be repoliticized. What we have been calling the political side of housing needs to be brought back into public discussions.

In practice, housing's political consequences are rarely clear-cut. Dwellings can be both oppressive and liberating at the same time. And because profits and power do not define all of life, oppression in housing can also hurt those who benefit from it. Even those who directly profit from the residential oppression of others can be harmed by those same conditions: their residential environments become guarded enclaves, their range of contacts and experiences is diminished, their self-perception is distorted. And to the extent that housing is used to bolster a political economic system that is crisis-prone and environmentally suicidal, residential oppression affects everyone.

The contradictions of residential politics stem from the contradictions of contemporary society. The situation can only be understood by exposing the process by which oppression in housing occurs, the people and interests that bring it about, the sources of resistance to it, and the liberating potential that lies within it. The fundamental questions about housing today are not about height restrictions or zoning changes, important as these questions can be. The core issues are what and whom housing is for, whom it oppresses, and whom it empowers.

4

The Myths of Housing Policy

Most discussions of housing policy operate on the assumption that, whether or not it has been successful, the state has tried to solve the housing question. That is, many accounts of housing politics are premised on the *myth of the benevolent state*. In brief, the myth is that government acts out of a primary concern for the welfare of all its citizens and that its policies represent an effort to find solutions to recognized social problems. If government efforts fall short of success, according to this narrative, it is only because of lack of knowledge, countervailing selfish interests, incompetence, or lack of courage.

The very term "housing policy" is evidence of this myth. The phrase itself suggests the existence of consistent governmental efforts to solve the housing problem. But a historical analysis of government actions and inactions affecting housing reveal nothing of the sort. Housing policy is an ideological artifact, not a real category. It is an artificially clear picture of what the state actually does in myriad uncoordinated and at times contradictory ways.

The actual motivations for state action in the housing sector have more to do with maintaining the political and economic order than with solving the housing crisis. If the state were truly concerned with the best course of action to meet society's dwelling needs and end residential oppression, housing history would look very different than it does.

To be sure, there is no conspiratorial, unified ruling class that controls the state in an unchallenged way. Even among elites, there are conflicts between different factions that have real political consequences. And popular pressure and social movements have shaped state outcomes in meaningful ways.[1]

But the state has usually found some way to neutralize radical challenges, especially concerning welfare and housing programs. Throughout American history, state policies have channeled system-challenging demands for the democratization of housing into system-maintaining form.[2] The result has been policies that, one way or another, reproduce the housing problem.

Historically, the state has used the housing system to preserve political stability and support the accumulation of private profit. They have been more or less prominent in different eras, but these two priorities are the hallmarks of state housing policy under capitalism. And they continue to explain state actions towards housing even today. An examination of some of the most influential low-income housing policies in the United States will show that the benevolent provision of dwelling space in order to solve the housing problem has never been the overriding goal.

---

1   See chapter five, this volume.

2   On "system-challenging" versus "system-maintaining," see Peter Marcuse, "Professional Ethics and Beyond: Values in Planning," *Journal of the American Institute of Planners* 42.3 (1976), 264–74.

The Politics of Housing Regulation

Although American "housing policy" is often narrated as beginning with New York's nineteenth-century tenement house reform, the state's role in regulating and stabilizing the housing system goes back much further. Detailed and extensive planning and public construction took place in colonial Williamsburg, Savannah, and Philadelphia. In 1766, New York adopted building regulations that created a fire zone in which houses had to be made of stone or brick and roofed with tile or slate. These early regulations were made in anticipation of growth and in realization of an increasingly complex web of interrelationships within cities. The Commissioner's Plan for New York of 1811, which laid out the gridiron street pattern in Manhattan, was drafted in order to facilitate circulation and to organize land speculation. It was one of the many ways that state action supported the production of private housing.

New York's adoption of the 1867 Tenement House Act, which required fire escapes, windows in every bedroom, and at least one toilet per twenty inhabitants, is often trotted out as evidence for the city's commitment to good housing for the poor. But contrary to the myth of state benevolence, the real reasons were elites' twin fears of disease and uprising among the city's growing working class.

The city's political establishment reacted with panic to the threat of social and economic instability stemming from the health problems of the poor. Smallpox, dysentery, tuberculosis, and other diseases were spawned in the tenement districts, but threatened to wreak havoc throughout the city. The New York Association for Improving the Condition of the Poor (AICP), led and financed by wealthy merchants and businessmen, called attention to the issue in 1843. According to the AICP, poverty was both "a massive threat to social stability" and "the direct consequence of individual depravity."[3] *Harper's Weekly* prophesied that without health laws "the City of New York will be left to its own destruction."[4] Tenement reform grew out of this genteel fear of the illnesses associated with poverty.

Fear of contagious disease was not the only driver of nineteenth-century housing regulation. There was also the perennial need to prevent uprisings. Throughout the nineteenth century, New Yorkers rioted on a regular basis. In the Astor Place riots of 1849, thousands raged outside a theater that was seen as a bastion of elitist culture; dozens were killed when the authorities opened fire on protesters, who were armed only with paving stones. The most famous and terrifying example was the Draft Riots of 1863, when anger at Civil War conscription policies that allowed the wealthy to buy their way out of military service turned into a series of racist and anti-immigrant pogroms, leaving 120 people dead. The Tompkins Square Riot of 1874 was until that point the largest demonstration that the city had ever seen. It involved a mass demonstration by thousands of workers, many of whom were members of the communist First International.

These are only some of the major incidents that defined an era of frequent uprising and public violence.[5] This unrest

---

3   Cited in Michael B. Katz, *In the Shadow of the Poorhouse: A Social History of Welfare in America* (New York: Basic Books, 1996 [1986]), 66.

4   Roy Lubove, *The Progressives and the Slums: Tenement House Reform in New York City, 1890–1917* (Pittsburgh: University of Pittsburgh Press, 1962), 23.

5   There were many other such uprisings. For example: sectarian rioting broke out on Christmas Day, 1806. Strikes by stevedores turned violent in 1825 and 1828, as did a strike by stonecutters in 1829. The weavers' strike of 1828 spurred violent marches and

embodied many clashing motivations, including anti-elitism, racism, nativism, and labor solidarity. Many of these incidents were not ignited by housing grievances, but they were exacerbated by the underlying dissatisfaction with intolerable day-to-day living conditions. The specter of public violence terrified the city's elites, and the fear of unrest played a key role in motivating the city's response to housing matters. The need to contain public discontent and maintain public order would be a factor, explicit or implicit, in all future housing policies.

Reformers were very clear that housing regulations were justified above all else by the self-interest of elites. The AICP warned in 1865 about the

> poverty and wretchedness of large masses of people . . . If left to themselves, there is a moral certainty that they will overrun the city as thieves and beggars—endanger public

---

industrial sabotage. Rioting and racist violence occurred in 1834 and 1835 surrounding the abolition of slavery. In 1837 New Yorkers took to the streets in response to the rising cost of flour. In 1870 and 1871, sectarian violence between Protestants and Catholics occurred alongside violence by and against the police. In 1886, sugar refinery workers in Williamsburg, Brooklyn, battled police officers and attacked delivery vehicles. A strike by streetcar operators in 1895 turned towards confrontation with the police and the destruction of infrastructure. See Paul A. Gilje, "Riots," pp. 1006–8 in Kenneth T. Jackson, ed., *The Encyclopedia of New York City* (New Haven, CT: Yale University Press, 1995), 1007; Sean Wilentz, *Chants Democratic: New York City and the Rise of the American Working Class, 1788–1850* (New York: Oxford University Press, 2004 [1980]), 169–70; Linda K. Kerber, "Abolitionists and Amalgamators: The New York City Race Riots of 1834," *New York History* 48.1 (1967) 28–39; J. T. Headley, *The Great Riots of New York* (New York: E. B. Treat, 1873).

peace and the security of property and life—tax the community for their support, and entail upon it an inheritance of vice and pauperism.[6]

Jacob Riis, the photographer and housing advocate who did much to publicize the housing problems of the Lower East Side, connected the violence against property committed during the Draft Riots to tenement conditions.[7] According to one historian, "The message to the city's propertied class was clear: ignore the housing needs of the property-less at the peril of your own property."[8] The reform movement also thought that better housing conditions would "reduce the class and ethnic conflict splitting the urban community into enemy camps," as well as provide a route to the Americanization of immigrant laborers.[9]

Emerging from these tense times and embodying the era's contradictions, the Tenement House Act of 1901 was the most significant chapter in the history of housing regulation in New York. It created the widespread inner-court layout typical of so many apartment buildings in the city (the so-called "new law" tenements). More so than its predecessors, the 1901 law did rein in some of the deadliest housing conditions. But it was aimed at

---

6   New York Association for the Improvement of the Poor, *The Thirteenth Annual Report* (New York: John F. Trow, 1856), 24.

7   Jacob A. Riis, *How the Other Half Lives: Studies among the Tenements of New York* (New York: Charles Scribner's Sons, 1924 [1890]), 2.

8   Robert E. Fogelsong, *Planning the Capitalist City: The Colonial Era to the 1920s* (Princeton, NJ: Princeton University Press, 1986), 77.

9   Lubove, *The Progressives and the Slums*, 43.

preserving New York's housing hierarchy and ameliorating its worst harms rather than transforming it. The law served as a precedent for a wave of similar legislation passed by other states in the following decades.

The adoption of the 1901 law was substantially due to the efforts of Lawrence Veiller. A well-known campaigner and public official, Veiller had done much to organize and professionalize the housing reform movement. He saw housing as a way to ensure that immigrants and the working class were integrated into the economic order:

> The modern city is the most important factor in destroying a conservative point of view on the part of the working people. Where a man has a home and owns it, he has an incentive to work industriously, to be economical and thrifty, to take an interest in public affairs; every tendency makes him conservative. But where a man's home is three or four rooms in some huge building in which dwell from twenty to thirty other families and this home is only his from month to month, what incentive is there to economy? What is there to develop a sense of civic responsibility or patriotism?[10]

For reformers like Veiller, housing was as much a tool for bolstering the social order as it was a way to soften the harshness of poverty. Housing was offered as a part of the solution to the general problem of controlling labor and instilling discipline.

---

10 Lawrence Veiller, "The Housing Problem in American Cities," *Annals of the American Academy of Political and Social Science* 25 (1905), 52–3.

Veiller, Riis, and the other housing advocates of the era were progressive reformers driven by a combination of motives. It is clear that liberals, idealists, philanthropists, and others working in charitable fields contributed to the passage of laws that prevented the most egregious housing conditions. But whatever their personal motivations, their actions also served the broad goals of New York's elites.

Viewed historically, tenement house regulations do not mark the beginning of benevolent governmental attitudes towards those who are poorly housed. They were animated by fear rather than by benevolence. And reformers did whatever they could to prevent more radical responses to the housing question; indeed, they saw the prevalence of radical political views, especially among immigrants, as one reason why housing reform was necessary. Housing regulation is an example of the state acting to protect the existing order from the economic and political dangers created by industrialization and urbanization. That these policies also benefited the poor was neither a necessary nor a sufficient cause of their enactment.

Public Provision of Housing

If regulation and building codes were not the beginnings of benevolent policies seeking to remedy residential problems, then neither was public housing. New York City was a pioneer both in housing regulation and later in municipal housing provision. But the development of the two was not connected, contrary to what the myth of the benevolent state might have us believe. And as with building regulations, the motivations behind early public housing programs had little to do with providing decent homes for the urban poor or emancipating them from their housing problems. Instead, the public provision of housing was used by the state as a tool to achieve other goals.

Lawrence Veiller opposed public housing vociferously. For Veiller, public housing meant unfair competition with private capital, and he argued that it promoted the growth of cumbersome and mechanical government systems. Almost all of the early US reformers agreed that "it was 'bad principle and worse policy' for municipalities 'to spend public money competing with private enterprise in housing the masses.'"[11] Some housing advocates, for example the prominent reformer and economist Edith Elmer Wood, did indeed see public housing, along with regulation, as central to a strategy to improve the housing conditions of the poor. The urbanist Catherine Bauer made the case for the public provision of dwellings in her book *Modern Housing*.[12] But their positions were sidelined.

Before the turn of the century, there had been a move towards the private philanthropic sponsorship of housing and the construction of model tenements on a charitable or limited-profit basis. But this movement did not galvanize widespread support or yield public housing legislation at the time. Government-sponsored housing construction only began when public housing overlapped with other goals of the state.

Rather than arising out of a benevolent concern for the poor, housing efforts were closely related to a series of military, economic, and political objectives. Some advocates, like Wood and Bauer, did indeed continue to fight for the social provision

---

11 Lubove, *The Progressives and the Slums*, 104; Anthony Jackson, *A Place Called Home: A History of Low-Cost Housing in Manhattan* (Cambridge, MA: MIT Press, 1976), 121.

12 Catherine Bauer, *Modern Housing* (Cambridge, MA: Houghton Mifflin, 1934).

of housing throughout this period. But the policies that actually produced early public housing had other sources. There were three major phases in the early history of public housing in the United States: the World War I programs, the postwar veterans' programs, and the public housing programs that followed the Great Depression. Though these policies have been interpreted as evidence of a growing benevolent state, they were largely discontinuous episodes.

The need to support sensitive wartime industries was the true origin of the earliest state-supported housing programs in America. During World War I, the US Shipping Board Emergency Fleet Corporation was created under the Shipping Act of 1916. Two years later it was given the authority to build or requisition housing for "employees and the families of employees of shipyards in which ships are being constructed for the United States." Later, in 1918, the US Housing Corporation was established to help "such industrial workers as are engaged in arsenals and navy yards of the United States and in industries connected with and essential to the national defense, and their families."[13]

Wartime industry was centered in a number of older American cities, all of which had serious housing shortages. As part of the war effort, the state lent its resources to the private companies involved in these strategic industries. Housing units were publicly owned when built, but a provision of the law mandated that they be sold to private owners soon after the war ended. The antecedent of these wartime efforts lies not in Progressive Era housing reform, but in the factory towns of the late nineteenth century. Paternalistic industrialists like

---

13   Lawrence Meir Friedman, *Government and Slum Housing: A Century of Frustration* (Chicago: Rand McNally, 1968), 95.

George Pullman were the actual forebears of public housing in the United States.

The next stage in the early history of public housing was the veterans' programs adopted after World War I by several American states. Veterans returned after the war to a massive housing shortage. Many faced poverty and homelessness. In response, some states provided subsidized loans to help them purchase private homes. The most ambitious of these programs was that of the state of California, which provided low-interest loans to more than 7,000 families through the Veterans' Farm and Home Purchase Act of 1921.[14] These efforts, supported on the federal level by President Herbert Hoover's "Own Your Home" campaign, were mainly geared towards spurring construction and displaying patriotism by supporting the troops. Whereas similar programs in England and Scotland directed postwar construction towards those areas with the most severe shortages, the American programs lacked such geographic targeting. With no regard for actual housing need, state money was funneled directly to the private market.

The passage of the Wagner-Steagall Housing Act of 1937 marks the third and final stage of this early history. The law created the United States Housing Authority (USHA) and facilitated large-scale public housing construction. Reformers played a much bigger role than in previous periods; for example, both Bauer and Wood worked for USHA. But it is clear that the guiding motivation behind the ramping up of public housing in the United States was to stem unrest among the swelling ranks of unemployed urban workers during the Great

---

14   Gail Radford, *Modern Housing in America: Policy Struggles in the New Deal Era* (Chicago: The University of Chicago Press, 1996), 44.

Depression—a task that was to be accomplished not through the provision of housing, but through the creation of construction jobs. To prevent large numbers of affordable housing units flooding the market, the Housing Act mandated that one substandard dwelling be demolished for every public housing unit created—a requirement that remained in place through the 1980s. The result was a public housing program carefully crafted to support, rather than compete with, private housing.

Contradictions of Urban Renewal

The limits of the liberal narrative about the benevolent state are illustrated most clearly by looking at the various state actions that came to be known as "urban renewal" or "slum clearance." The consequences of slum clearance as practiced in the United States after 1949 are well known.[15] The program was criticized, correctly, as destroying more housing than it produced. It displaced the poor to make room for the rich, and used public funds to redevelop valuable land near central business districts for the benefit of downtown merchants, property owners, and the business community.

But the standard critiques do not go far enough. Most such

---

15   See Christopher Klemek, *The Transatlantic Collapse of Urban Renewal: Postwar Urbanism from New York to Berlin* (Chicago: The University of Chicago Press, 2011); Jon C. Teaford, "Urban Renewal and Its Aftermath," *Housing Policy Debate* 11.2 (2000), 443–65; Jewel Bellush and Murray Hausknecht, eds, *Urban Renewal: People, Politics, and Planning* (Garden City, NY: Doubleday, 1976); James Q. Wilson, ed., *Urban Renewal: The Record and the Controversy* (Cambridge, MA: MIT Press, 1966).

criticism in the United States refers to the "failures of urban renewal."[16] The critics speak as if the ravages of slum clearance were perversions of its original benevolent intent—as if insufficient foresight or unanticipated changes in patterns of urban development had led to these consequences. Even radical critics of the program often saw it as being diverted from its original purpose by local business cliques and real estate interests. In fact, urban renewal was decisively shaped by the agendas of the real estate and finance industries from the beginning.

The legislative basis for urban renewal was the Housing Act of 1949. The law mainly accomplished two things: it reinstituted the New Deal public housing program, which had been dormant since World War II, and provided financing for slum clearance.[17] Title I, the part of the law that established the urban development program, was seen by its proponents as a means of strengthening downtown and eliminating the sight of urban decay nearby. Supporters were not concerned with aiding those who were poorly housed but with tearing down areas they considered to be slums—at least those located near major business centers. They focused as much on the redevelopment of nonresidential areas as they did on housing. The very groups who were the strongest opponents of public housing in the United States—the National Association of Real Estate Boards, the United States Savings and Loan League (USSLL), and, to some extent, the Mortgage Bankers Association of America—still supported the basic principle of urban redevelopment. Testimony on behalf of USSLL argued, "Our people have

---

16   Wilson, *Urban Renewal.*

17   See Alexander von Hoffman, "A Study in Contradictions: The Origins and Legacy of the Housing Act of 1949," *Housing Policy Debate* 11.2 (200), 299–326.

studied the problem of slum clearance for some years and agree that it is an appropriate field for public action and public expenditure. We have felt that the procedure could be carried out largely by local governments and that, after the land so acquired was written down to a reasonable use value, it should be used for its highest and best use, public or private."[18]

Urban renewal also drew support from planners, architects, and urbanists. One of the major supporters of the slum clearance agenda was the American Institute of Planners and especially its president, Alfred Bettman, a nationally known promoter of zoning. Another major supporter was the Urban Land Institute, a planning research organization sponsored by developers. Both organizations specifically opposed statutory requirements stating that urban renewal only be used to redevelop residential land and then reused after clearance only for housing purposes. They slowly succeeded: first 10 percent, then 20 percent of projects were exempted from the original mandate that redeveloped land be reserved for housing. The requirement, in any event, only stipulated that post-renewal uses be "predominantly" residential—a formulation that the imaginative drawing of project boundaries could render ineffectual. As one legal commentator lamented, a major reason for this mission creep, which flew in the face of the benevolent rhetoric of the 1949 law, was

> the position of business interests which normally tend to support restrictions on federal expenditures, but are increasingly in favor of reconstructing blighted businesses and industrial properties. Foremost among these are department store owners and mortgage and other lenders concerned about large outstanding investments in

---

18   Cited in Wilson, *Urban Renewal*, 81–2.

downtown retail properties, now suffering competition from suburban shopping centers.[19]

As slum clearance rolled out in cities across the country, its list of supporters grew. The program was eventually promoted by a wide range of business interests: major commercial banks, legal and accounting firms, the headquarters of national and international corporations, and other outfits with an interest in downtown locations.

Even while urban renewal had the solid support of business and political leaders, it was uprooting entire working-class neighborhoods and communities of color. Across the United States from the 1950s until 1980, an estimated one million households were displaced.[20] Eventually the organized resistance of those who were removed was so powerful it could no longer be ignored. Either the process would grind to a halt altogether, or the protesters would have to be accommodated. Residents won increases in relocation benefits, improvements in administration, and obligations to construct replacement housing for the displaced. These changes were not the result of a reawakened commitment to fighting residential injustice; rather, they showed what effective protest could accomplish.

If mid-century housing policies were actually evolving to meet housing need, one would expect to find the numbers of new construction starts to be increasing as housing need increased and declining as need declined. But while the housing shortage was at its most dire, steadily growing from 1930 through about 1949,

---

19   Ibid., 113.

20   Herbert J. Gans, *People, Plans and Policies: Essays on Poverty, Racism, and Other National Urban Problems* (New York: Columbia University Press, 1993), 213.

public housing production was at a low point. New housing units saw their greatest growth during the 1950s, when the housing shortage was declining overall.[21] Housing need and the production of new units through urban renewal did not correlate.

Not only did urban renewal consistently fail to address the housing crisis; in many ways, slum clearance made the housing crisis worse. Mortgage insurance and public expenditures on highways and other infrastructure added up to a massive public subsidy for postwar suburbanization. Far from aiding the poor, this effort undermined urban neighborhoods. Downtown jobs began disappearing, harming municipal budgets. Public services were reduced. The consequences of racial segregation and inequality were amplified. Public housing, on the other hand, the only housing program directly providing shelter for the poor, was hobbled from the beginning. The activists and advocates who were pushing for ways out of public housing's "dreary deadlock" were ignored.[22]

Public Policy and Private Profit

The housing programs that were enacted in the wake of urban renewal aided private developers in an even more direct way.

---

21   This claim draws on figures from the US Bureau of the Census, *Historical Statistics of the United States: Colonial Times to 1970* (Washington: Government Publishing Office, 1975); US Department of Housing and Urban Development, *Housing in the Seventies* (Washington: Government Publishing Office, 1976); Henry J. Aaron, *Shelter and Subsidies: Who Benefits from Federal Housing Policies?* (Washington: Brookings Institution, 1972).

22   Catherine Bauer Wurster, "The Dreary Deadlock of Public Housing," *Architectural Forum* 106 (1957), 140–2, 219–22.

Urban renewal facilitated real estate capital's goals, but it also included a strong role for the state as planner and coordinator. After urban renewal, the state largely restricted itself to providing funds for projects controlled by private firms. The process by which housing policy was privatized exemplifies what Manuel Castells calls "the constant tendency . . . to make the sectors of public subsidization profitable in order to bring them into line with the criteria of private capital so as to be able to transfer them gradually over to it."[23] In other words, public support for housing construction for families below the level of economically effective demand was conditioned upon finding a way to make it serve private profit.

The first step away from state control over urban renewal was the turnkey construction process, which permitted private builders to do all of the construction on their own land and then sell the completed development to public authorities. Developers were able to profit both from the construction work and from the increase in land prices. The second step was the perfection of the limited-dividend tax-benefit approach, which permitted private interests not only to build privately on public land but also to continue to own and manage the publicly subsidized housing that they built. In exchange for some limits on profit, real estate companies enjoyed significant tax benefits.

The next step was the Section 8 voucher program established through the Housing Act of 1974. Section 8 permits private

---

23   Manuel Castells, "Neo-capitalism, Collective Consumption and Urban Contradictions: New Sources of Inequality and New Models of Change," conference paper, Models of Change in Advanced Industrial Societies, Monterosso al Mare (November 1973), 12.

interests to build, own, and manage housing intended for the poor, with no limits on profit whatsoever beyond those nominally imposed by a requirement that rents be based on an administratively determined level. The state supports rent payments to private owners through subsidies based on the occupants' income. With vouchers, private actors have fully retaken the task of low-income housing provision from the state. Indeed, vouchers are a way to expand the reach of the housing market by subsidizing tenants who would otherwise not be able to afford market-rate rents. The clear beneficiary is the private landlord.

The low-income housing policies created in the 1980s continued the pattern. The Low-Income Housing Tax Credit (LIHTC), introduced in 1986, allocates tax credits to private developers.[24] The credits are then typically resold to investors. While the budget for public housing was disappearing, funding for LIHTC steadily increased. The tax credit provides numerous advantages for its corporate beneficiaries. Under LIHTC, "corporate investors earn substantial profits . . . typically a 15 percent return on equity and they, in turn, become part of a powerful lobbying group."[25] After fifteen years, most dwellings created using the LIHTC are able to revert to market rents.

Using tax subsidies to fund low-income housing is politically convenient for the government. Because it is implemented using

---

24   Tax credits are offset against the final tax otherwise due, dollar for dollar. They are thus worth much more than simple tax abatements or exemptions, since they reduce the actual tax paid, not just the income on the basis of which the tax is computed.

25   Peter Dreier, "Federal Housing Subsidies: Who Benefits and Why?," pp. 105–38 in Rachel G. Bratt, Michael E. Stone, and Chester Hartman, eds, *A Right to Housing: Foundation for a New Social Agenda* (Philadelphia: Temple University Press, 2006), 120.

the tax code rather than through the budget of a federal agency, a tax credit's costs do not appear as such on government ledgers. But it surrenders a fundamental social welfare issue to control by private interests.

Today, the keyword is "affordable housing." The exemplar of this approach is a program called inclusionary zoning. It was central to the housing policy of New York's former mayor Michael Bloomberg, and forms the core of the housing plan adopted by Bloomberg's successor, Bill de Blasio. The strategy takes different forms, but the basic idea is that in exchange for the right to build more market-rate housing than would be allowed under existing zoning law, private developers agree to construct some number of nominally "affordable" units as well. The non-market-rate dwellings provided through these programs are sited and designed by real estate developers with minimal regulation. Under some version of the programs, they may be located off-site, some miles away. And under most versions of inclusionary zoning, non-market-rate units may revert to market rate after a specified period.

Inclusionary zoning's supporters justify it as a benevolent program to provide housing for those who cannot afford it. It is thought that connecting market-rate development with subsidized units is a way to maintain economic diversity in housing. The program's very name suggests that it is the opposite of "exclusionary zoning," which uses land-use regulations to enforce segregation.

Some inclusionary housing strategies are better crafted than others. And there may be reasons to support such policies in some instances.[26] But seen in historical context, inclusionary

---

26   See Peter Marcuse, "Blog #50. Inclusionary Zoning: Good and Bad," *PMarcuse.wordpress.com*, May 15, 2014; Peter Marcuse,

zoning appears, like many programs before it, to meet the needs of real estate more than the housing needs of residents.

In New York, the most obvious issue with this kind of program is affordability. Definitions of income eligibility for these programs are based on percentages of a measurement called "area median income." This figure is calculated for an entire metropolitan region, throwing detached suburban single-family homes into the average along with less expensive mass housing. For eligibility purposes, the area median income for New York is currently $86,300 for a family of four. But according to the US Census Bureau, the actual average annual income for households in New York City is $52,737; that figure for the Bronx is less than $35,000. The result is that many units of "affordable" housing are not affordable for large numbers of working-class or poor people.

When so-called affordable housing programs are producing apartments that are priced at levels virtually identical to what developers would demand without the affordability requirement, it is clear that the term "affordable" is not descriptive so much as ideological. Rather than an actual attempt to address residential problems, affordable housing policies in cities like New York today are tools to legitimize state support for luxury development. Promoters of inclusionary zoning and other affordable housing programs cast them as pragmatic solutions to the housing crisis. But in practice, despite the best intentions of some of its advocates, affordable housing is more of a strategy of the real estate machine than a relief from it.

"Blog #53. Density, Inclusionary Zoning, Housing Planning: Cautions on de Blasio's Plan," *PMarcuse.wordpress.com*, July 1, 2014.

With affordable housing, as with nearly all privatized lower-income housing plans, there is virtually no connection between the housing on offer and the actual residential needs of working-class households. The below-market apartments are provided by the private market where and when it is profitable for it to do so. And they are distributed based on waiting lists or, more often, lotteries. In 2014, there were 2,500 below-market apartments on offer via lotteries in New York—and 1.5 million applications for them.[27] Acquiring such a unit is in essence a matter of luck. There is no sense in which affordable housing is in touch with the ideal of housing as a right of social citizenship.

New York's housing movements have recognized the contradictions of affordable housing, and many have organized protests against the strategy. Numerous activist groups and coalitions have mobilized in opposition to rezoning plans based around the inclusionary principle. Activists have been particularly concerned to highlight how affordable housing is being used to facilitate gentrification. Protests against inclusionary housing in places like East Harlem or Greenpoint have sought to disrupt what one geographer calls the "general consensus in which real estate–led development is regarded not as a cause of gentrification but as its solution."[28]

Housing policy has consistently been designed to meet the economic needs of the real estate industry and the political needs

27   Mireya Navarrojan, "Long Lines, and Odds, for New York's Subsidized Housing Lotteries," *New York Times*, January 29, 2015.

28   Filip Stabrowski, "Inclusionary Zoning and Exclusionary Development: The Politics of 'Affordable Housing' in North Brooklyn," forthcoming in *International Journal of Urban and Regional Research* 3.

of those running the state. It is a matter of historical fact that housing programs in the United States have almost never been designed around actually addressing the housing crisis. A responsive state, much less a benevolent one, has only been a footnote in the history of American housing policy.

The Myth of the Meddling State

The story of a benevolent state doing its best to solve housing problems was used to justify more than a century of market-friendly liberalism. But since the 1980s, there has been a competing, conservative narrative about housing policy: the myth of the meddling state. It is in many ways the mirror image of the tale of the benevolent state. And it is just as inaccurate.

For believers in the meddling state, housing policy is an unbroken chain of failure. From this perspective, a fully private, minimally regulated market will produce the best of all possible housing outcomes. Market interaction reveals both the cost of supply and the levels of effective demand. Where the supply and demand curves intersect is the optimal level of production. If supply does not respond adequately, the problem lies with government regulation that hinders its free operations. To achieve this optimal housing situation, the removal, not the improvement, of regulation is required. The state is unneeded and counterproductive. The conclusion: get the government out of housing.

The implications of the myth of the meddling state for government policy are clear: on the demand side, if all else fails, transfer payments in the form of vouchers, or, preferably, massive amounts of debt; on the supply side, freedom from government regulation. The latter, in fact, should take priority over the former: in this view, demand will ultimately take care of itself. Those who really want to work can get jobs, and if they do not want to work, they do not want to make the trade-off necessary to get decent housing, so they are not morally entitled to it.

The idea of a meddling state ignores two major facts. The first is quite simple: all of the federal money spent on public housing and other direct subsidies for working-class and poor households pales in comparison to the money spent subsidizing wealthy and middle-class homeowners. Tax expenditures constitute over three-fourths of the government's total housing subsidies, including tax deductions for mortgage payments, deductions on property tax payments, and deferral of capital gains taxes on real estate sales. The vast majority of these credits are claimed by taxpayers in the highest income bracket.[29] If the state has been "interfering" with housing, it has been doing so by substantially lowering the costs of homeownership for people who can already afford it. The idea that what the state has done, it has done in the interests of the poor is standing history on its head.

Second, and more importantly, the picture of government interference implies a false account of the relationship between housing and the state. It posits the state as an alien intruder into an autonomous housing market. The market is imagined as a rational sphere that operates more efficiently the less the state intervenes, and which would operate perfectly if the state left it alone entirely.

In fact, housing has always been dependent upon, and integrally tied to, state action. The government is involved in making housing possible in multiple ways. The state plans and builds the streets on which homes are located. It certifies the

29   Dreier, "Federal Housing Subsidies," 107–11.

materials and techniques out of which houses are constructed. It regulates, or directly supplies, the infrastructure for electricity, water, sewage, and transportation upon which housing depends. It provides the means to enforce contracts and define the legal relationships that make possible the buying, selling, producing, and leasing of housing. It enforces the legal sanctity of the home from intrusion and violation. It constructs and protects the property rights that make landlordism and tenancy possible. It influences the extent to which capital is used for housing or diverted from it.

Government does not intervene in an autonomous private housing market. The state can more accurately be said to privilege some groups or classes over others. It can take a stronger or weaker position regarding particular residential issues. But it does not intervene in an essentially separate sphere. In a sense, all housing is public housing, in that all housing is shaped by public action and depends upon public authority—and indeed, many housing units have received tax benefits or some other form of direct or indirect public subsidy as well.[30] None of this is to suggest that the state has unlimited legitimacy within the sphere of housing, or that state action cannot be criticized. Of course it can, and should. But calls for the state to get out of housing markets are incoherent. The housing system is inextricably tied to the state, law, and public authority. The question will always be *how* the state should act towards housing, not whether it should do so.

In fact, by pretending that the state is a foreign agent trespassing on the sovereign market, the narrative of the meddling

---

30   Cf. Reinhold Martin, ed., *Public Housing: A New Conversation* (New York: Buell Center for the Study of American Architecture, 2009), 13.

state prevents the development of a more critical view of what the government actually does in the housing system. If the state is always an intruder, differences between policy alternatives become hard to decipher. And the role of the state in establishing and protecting the residential status quo becomes concealed.

The political and economic purposes of the myth of the meddling state are clear, and blatant: to justify the reduction of expenditures for social and redistributive programs; to make it easier to kill any statute limiting the freedom of the private sector to make a profit; and to close the already small space for the creation of an alternative, decommodified housing sector. From a point of view that examines how states and housing actually work, it is hard to take the meddling state story seriously. From a practical, political view, however, it has proven very useful to its beneficiaries. Getting rid of the meddling state does not mean "getting government out of housing." It means using government to reproduce residential inequalities.

Housing Politics without Myths

The state is not a neutral organization. Nor is it a fully united and coherent one. Understanding the role of the government in housing requires a clear view of the conflicts and struggles in which states are actually involved. In the United States, state power has consistently been used to reinforce rather than dismantle social hierarchy. But in different hands and under different circumstances, the state could be a vehicle for real housing alternatives. Both of the myths we have discussed obscure this point.

It must be stressed that in misunderstanding government policy, a view of housing politics that relies upon either of these myths also misunderstands the market. The liberal narrative recognizes that markets in housing can contribute to housing problems, but it fails to grasp just how often programs nominally designed to alleviate residential suffering do in fact function to enrich private developers. In contrast, the conservative myth of the meddling state simply ignores the consequences of the commodification of housing and sees market provision as automatically preferable to public action regardless of its consequences. Fundamentally, both of these positions fail to see markets clearly.

The debate must move beyond the shallow idea that the housing question comes down to determining the right balance between state and market. Seeing the issue in these simple terms does not work. State action can be used to democratize and redistribute housing, or it can function to preserve inequality and support private profitmaking. Rather than relying upon either the myth of the benevolent state or that of the meddling state, we need to see who actually sets government policy and whose interests are really served by it.

5

Housing Movements of New York

On the night of June 29, 2015, hundreds of tenants and activists gathered at Cooper Union's Great Hall near Astor Place in Manhattan. They were assembled to witness a vote by the Rent Guidelines Board, which regulates the rents of New York's more than one million rent-stabilized leases. Since it was founded in 1969, the board had voted to increase rents every year. But this year was different. Skyrocketing rents, sympathetic press coverage, a well-organized campaign involving dozens of groups throughout the city, and a new and supportive mayor meant that the voice of tenants was louder than it had been in years.

The board voted not to permit rent raises on one-year leases. Tenants rejoiced. Landlords were outraged and called the move "unconscionable."[1] In fact, New York's landlords were as

---

1   Mireya Navarro, "New York City Board Votes to Freeze Regulated Rents on One-Year Leases," *New York Times*, June 29, 2015.

powerful as ever.[2] But the 2015 rent freeze showed that in a city ruled by real estate, tenant power was alive and kicking.

Who decides what housing is to be provided, at what price, for whom and where? The two most powerful actors, the real estate industry and the state, have never had absolute control over the housing system. They have always had to contend, one way or another, with the power of housing's inhabitants, particularly when they take the form of organized housing movements.

Housing movements are popular struggles by those for whom housing means home, not real estate.[3] They mobilize on behalf, in the phrase from Henri Lefebvre, of "all those who *inhabit*."[4] In theory this could include everyone. But in practice, inhabitants have multiple identities: as workers, professionals, renters, owner-occupiers, migrants, members of particular racial or ethnic communities, etc. As a consequence, movements focused on housing can take a near-infinite number of forms. Throughout

---

2   As evidenced, as many activists pointed out, by the fact that the rent freeze did not even cover two-year leases; see below.

3   This chapter is focused on New York. For a consideration of national-scale movements, see Peter Dreier, "The Tenant's Movement in the United States," *International Journal of Urban and Regional Research* 8.2 (1984), 255–79. On the UK, see Quintin Bradley, *The Tenants Movement: Resident Involvement, Community Action and the Contentious Politics of Housing* (London: Routledge, 2014). On urban movements in a global perspective, see Pierre Hamel, Henri Lustiger-Thaler, and Margit Mayer, eds, *Urban Movements in a Globalising World* (London: Routledge, 2003).

4   Henri Lefebvre, "The Right to the City," pp. 63–181 in Eleonore Kofman and Elizabeth Lebas, eds and trans., *Writings on Cities* (Malden, MA: Blackwell, 1996 [1967]), 158, emphasis in original.

their history, they exhibit enormous variety in terms of tactics, strategies, goals, alliances, political calculations, compromises, and ideologies.

Despite these differences, however, all forms of housing activism share a common purpose: the defense of the home and the personal lifeworld against economic pressures. Housing movements fight for use values against exchange values; for residential interests against the interests of landlords, banks, developers, and investors; for housing as home against the other economic and political ends for which housing has been appropriated.

What are the typical goals of housing movements? How have these goals been pursued? What power do the users of dwelling space really have? These questions are important for both theory and practice. No account of the housing system is complete without an understanding of the collective power of inhabitants. Activists never win everything that they demand. But state actions towards housing have indeed been influenced by their actions, and sometimes even by the mere threat of their organizing.

Housing Movements and the City

New York does not typify all cities. But the history of housing movements there shows a number of typical characteristics. In New York, as in many other cities, housing movements have come in waves. They rise, crest, and disperse. But they are never stamped out. Many social movements follow this cyclical pattern, but it is particularly strong in the case of housing movements. Housing struggles aimed at systemic change are inherently long-term. But individual households most often mobilize in response to immediate emergencies like evictions, rent increases, or environmental catastrophe. A household fights eviction, wins a long-term lease, and loses much of its incentive to keep fighting on less pressing issues. This is a problem for housing movements, even as it also fuels them.

Housing organizations tend to morph and recombine. There have long been attempts to organize permanent coalitions, but none have proven durable. Housing groups form and re-form coalitions with each other and with activists working on other causes, such as antiracism, welfare rights, consumer rights, immigrant rights, public health, feminist, and LGBT issues as particular social questions become prominent and as different groups move through the housing system.

One source of churn within movements is the complexity of structural positions within the housing system. Tenants have clashed with landlords, homeowners have struggled with banks, developers have fought with public housing residents, construction workers have mobilized against property owners, and speculators have created problems for tenants and nonprofit housing groups. These conflicts are mostly local and intermittent, but are sometimes reflected at higher levels, as in fights over state or national legislation.

Housing movements have consistently faced questions about whom to target. Focus has shifted from direct confrontation between private forces in the housing field—mainly tenants versus landlords—to pressures for state action, and shifted back again. The focus has varied from period to period and movement to movement. At high points in mobilization cycles, the two have tended to merge.

Movements have also been divided over what to demand. They have always fought against displacement and oppression, and for accessibility and security. But they have operationalized these ambitions in different ways depending upon political circumstances.

Activists have had an ambivalent and shifting relationship with other political actors involved in the housing question. Residential struggles have been both supported and constrained by the work of philanthropists, intellectuals, professionals, social workers, and health advocates, and by those active in "good-government" efforts for whom housing reform was linked to broader concerns like public health and social order. Professional social reformers, especially, have long been strong allies for housing activists. They have provided crucial links to powerful institutions and elite decision-makers. But they have also sought to change movement goals and the manner in which they are pursued.

Residential protest has also been marked by questions surrounding the place of ownership in the housing system. The pursuit of homeownership as a means of solving housing problems on an individual basis, supported by long-standing and widely shared ideological positions, often resulted in organized action, sometimes supporting but often weakening more collectively oriented efforts at housing change. Owner-occupiers are inhabitants too, but they have a financial and political stake in the housing system that itself varies historically. In general, the quest for homeownership has been a factor limiting the potential of housing as an organizing issue and dividing those with a stake in its resolution. This connection is found across the world but has been more pronounced in the United States than in almost any other country.

Housing movements in New York have often been led by women. As movements that politicize social reproduction and consumption, it is only logical that they have drawn strength from those relegated to laboring in those spheres. Women have provided tenant's groups with organizational and ideological leadership as well as rank-and-file strength. This is a characteristic shared with housing movements across the world.

Housing politics also tend to overlap with racial and ethnic politics. Communities of color, ethnic associations, civil rights organizations, antiracist activists, and others fighting for racial and ethnic justice have targeted residential discrimination and inequality. The overlap of housing with racial and ethnic constituencies makes it difficult to distinguish between movements to democratize housing and movements for racial equality. For marginalized groups, the demand for adequate housing has been part of the fundamental demand for dignity. This is also a characteristic shared with housing movements across the world.

Can one, then, speak with historical accuracy of a singular, distinct housing movement in New York, in which a coherent set of actors consistently pursued a common goal? No. Housing activism in New York City has been discontinuous and diverse. But it has never disappeared.

Pre-history of New York Housing Movements

Struggles over housing evolved from struggles over land. Until the nineteenth century, the housing question in New York was still essentially a question of production, related to rents paid as a share of crop yields rather than rents for the right to occupy housing. The two were not separately treated in law or in practice. Anti-eviction tactics of tenants necessarily protested eviction from homes as well as evictions from livelihoods. But the security of workers, rather than of residents, lay at the heart of the conflict. Housing movements were thus prototypically rural movements.

Opposition to renter status occasionally surfaced as a demand in urban labor struggles. In the 1820s, Thomas Skidmore, a New York City labor leader, advocated the abolition of rent and a universal right to landownership. But he seems to have been a lone voice, and was ousted from his position in the labor movement in part because of the radicalism of his ideas on property ownership. He stands in the tradition that includes the National Reform Association, organized in 1844, and later the political economist Henry George, who ran unsuccessfully for mayor of New York in 1886. Both Skidmore and George saw the land question as a mechanism to redress economic justice in general, rather than as a housing issue per se. And they saw changed conditions of ownership as the solution to social inequality.[5]

In the first half of the nineteenth century, housing was becoming a critical issue. In the aftermath of the economic crisis of 1837, unemployment spiked, poorhouses were filled, and eviction was an imminent threat to hundreds of thousands of people. Rent, food, and other necessities became unaffordable. Attacks on landlords for rent gouging and exploitation were frequent. Posters in support of a demonstration in February 1837 declared, "BREAD, MEAT, RENT, FUEL! THEIR PRICES MUST COME DOWN! The voice of people shall be heard, and will prevail!"[6] Rent was no

---

5   Thomas Skidmore, *The Rights of Man to Property!* (New York: Alexander Ming Jr., 1829). See Steven J. Ross, "The Culture of Political Economy: Henry George and the American Working Class," *Southern California Quarterly* 65.2 (1983), 145–66; Edward Pessen, "Thomas Skidmore, Agrarian Reformer in the Early American Labor Movement," *New York History* 35.3 (1954), 280–96.

6   Cited in Allan David Heskin, "The History of Tenants in the United States: Struggle and Ideology," *International Journal of Urban and Regional Research* 5.2 (1981), 190.

longer part of agrarian production. Now it was an urban issue. And landownership offered a target around which a number of different interests could converge: labor organizations, tenants, populist political leaders, and economic reformers.

The popular politics of housing in the early United States found its most militant expression in the anti-rent movements of the first half of the nineteenth century. New York State's Anti-Rent Movement lasted for some twenty years, from 1839 to 1859, and involved 300,000 tenants and 2,000,000 acres of land.[7] Tenant farmers on large landed estates in the Hudson Valley demanded the ownership of the land they occupied. They formed armed bands to resist evictions and physically prevented sheriffs from ousting families. They founded an organization to endorse candidates for public office, sued landlords contesting their title, and lobbied the state legislature for favorable laws protecting tenants. Ultimately, the Anti-Rent Movement won sufficient legal protections to force many landlords to sell their land at favorable prices and eliminate the worst abuses of the landlord–tenant relationship.

In 1844, Irish tenants and housing reformers organized a group called the Tenant League in New York City, the first movement in the United States specifically focused on housing as a distinct issue. They denounced the complex "system of landlordism" that then ruled New York as "one of the most blighted curses that ever was inflicted on the human race."[8] The

---

7   Charles W. McCurdy, *The Anti-Rent Era in New York Politics, 1839–1865* (Chapel Hill, NC: University of North Carolina Press, 2001); Heskin, "The History of Tenants in the United States"; Henry Christman, *Tin Horns and Calico: A Decisive Episode in the Emergence of Democracy* (New York: Holt, 1945).

8   Elizabeth Blackmar, *Manhattan for Rent, 1785–1850* (Ithaca, NY: Cornell University Press, 1989), 247.

Tenant League raised for the first time a demand that would become a centerpiece of most organized housing movements of the twentieth century: the control, in the name of fairness and the public good, of rents in privately owned accommodation.

The Birth of the Radical Tenant Movement

Housing movements in New York emerged as distinct from land reform movements with the development of industrial urbanism and the intensification of urbanization. As the city developed a complex industrial economy in the late nineteenth century, the number of tenants steadily increased. The growth of working-class renters had been steady since the founding of the city, but the period from 1890 to 1910 saw a huge jump in the numbers. The era's housing conditions were extensively documented by pioneers of urban photography like Jacob Riis, leading to waves of protest and reformist crusades.[9]

New York's tenants—schooled in industrial organizing, and often with backgrounds in European revolutionary politics—created the first movements that directly contested

---

9   A whole series of city, state, and finally (in 1903) federal studies provided both figures and descriptions of shocking conditions. And Jacob Riis's journalistic forays into the Lower East Side, for instance, sold hundreds of thousands of newspapers in New York City and brought to general attention the conditions under which poor tenants lived in the city. United States Bureau of Labor, *The Housing of the Working People* (Washington, DC: Government Printing Office, 1895); Jacob A. Riis, *How the Other Half Lives: Studies among the Tenements of New York* (New York: C. Scribner's and Sons, 1903); Jacob A. Riis, *The Battle with the Slums* (New York: Macmillan, 1902).

the structures of housing provision in the city. Early twentieth-century tenant politics was militant, organized, and effective. Waves of protest targeted both private landlords and the state, demanding rent rollbacks and regular maintenance from the former and tenant protections and public housing from the latter.

The first documented direct action by organized tenants occurred in the Lower East Side of Manhattan in 1904.[10] The neighborhood, largely home to working-class Eastern European Jewish garment workers, was expensive. According to one resident, the tenants of Lower East Side "lived and worked for the landlord."[11] And it was crowded; the area was said to be the most densely populated place on the planet. Rents had been increasing steadily for years, and many families had already been displaced to neighborhoods farther afield. That year, landlords decided to take advantage of the housing shortage by raising rents by an extra 20 to 30 percent.[12]

Every year on May 1, leases expired and landlords announced rent increases, a much-feared ritual known as "moving day." But that April, hundreds of families refused to pay the increased rent. They picketed their landlords' homes and took to the streets in protest marches. The strikers spread the word that no

---

10   Ronald Lawson, "The Rent Strike in New York City, 1904–1980: The Evolution of a Social Movement Strategy," *Journal of Urban History* 10.3 (1984), 237.

11   Jenna Weissman Joselit, "The Landlord as Czar: Pre-World War I Tenant Activity," pp. 39–50 in Ronald Lawson with Mark Naison, eds, *The Tenant Movement in New York City, 1904–1984* (New Brunswick, NJ: Rutgers University Press, 1986), 39.

12   Ibid.

new tenants should move into buildings owned by landlords who refused to negotiate.[13]

The impetus for the 1904 rent strike came from a successful consumer movement two years earlier. Jewish women had led a boycott of kosher butchers and succeeded in reversing price increases for meat in the city. Having proven its effectiveness, the same tool was used to fight rent increases. It also drew strength from the trade union movement and radical political parties. To support the strike the Social Democratic Party held a rally where a speaker declared, "Just as long as you continue to make laws whereby capitalists own everything that can be called the necessities of life, conditions will be unchanged."[14] The very terms "rent strike" and "tenant's union" attest to the connections to labor politics. Nonparticipating residents were derided as "scabs."[15]

The strike succeeded in its short-term goals. The courts were generally lenient. Landlords had threatened eviction against nonpaying tenants, but most did not keep their threat and many

---

13   The Lower East Side is rightly seen as the center of tenant activity at this time, but in May 1904 the action spread to Harlem, where signs appeared in windows announcing "This House Is on Strike" and many families stopped paying rent. See "Eighty Families on Strike for Low Rent," *New York Times*, May 17, 1904; "A Rent War in Harlem," *New York Times*, May 18, 1904.

14   "Anti-high Renters Plan Big Parade," *New York Times*, April 7, 1904.

15   Roberta Gold, *When Tenants Claimed the City: The Struggle for Citizenship in New York City Housing* (Urbana: University of Illinois Press, 2014), 13; Joselit, "The Landlord as Czar," 41. Not only were picket-line crossers denounced as scabs; successful rent strikers, in negotiations with their landlords, would not uncommonly demand that the scabs be evicted.

rolled back their rents. However, the formal organization set up by tenants, the New York Rent Protective Association, was short-lived. A socialist faction that wanted to broaden the struggle seceded, and the organization itself soon dissolved. The rapid formation and equally rapid disintegration of tenant organizations came to be a hallmark of the city's housing movements.

The second great wave of New York rent strikes took place against the backdrop of the Depression of 1907. Now the Socialist Party took the initiative in the organization, and gave the rent war a stronger ideological flavor. At one tenant rally on East Broadway, a mostly Yiddish-speaking crowd was exhorted to resist not only landlordism but also capitalism. One speaker declared,

> This is the richest and best developed country in the world. Who made it so? The rich? No. The Police Commissioner? No. The poor made it so. The only cure for this rent evil and all these evils is socialism. We must work together, one for all, all for one. Down with the rents![16]

Red flags—actually petticoats that had been dyed red—hung from the tenant strikers' windows.[17] But the anticapitalist rhetoric enabled a swell of anticommunist sentiment to be whipped up against them, and at the request of landlords, the courts issued several thousand eviction notices, effectively breaking the strike.

The next major wave of mobilization, which lasted from 1917 to 1920, was perhaps the largest and most radical housing

---

16   "Rent Strike Grows; Landlords Resist," *New York Times*, December 31, 1907.

17   Joselit, "The Landlord as Czar," 46.

uprising in New York's history. The movement was broader than in the past, involving not only Jewish families but also Italian and Irish tenants in Brooklyn, Harlem, and the Lower East Side.[18]

Housing insurrection seized New York. At a mass meeting in Beethoven Hall on East 5th Street,[19] Baruch Charney Vladeck, the labor leader, journalist, and Socialist member of the city's Board of Aldermen, called for a citywide rent strike. If every building on every block was organized, he argued, the courts and marshals would be overwhelmed and overpowered. Vladeck proclaimed, "Call it Bolshevism or anarchism, but I call it one of the tenets of real Americanism, when the people of the city get together to better their conditions." Jacob Panken, Socialist Party member and municipal judge, urged the crowd to take over the under-occupied luxury buildings of Fifth Avenue and Riverside Drive. "Just as the Government had the power to conscript life so can New York conscript these dwelling places," he argued.[20]

A series of tenant unions were formed throughout the city: first in Washington Heights, followed by Williamsburg,

---

18   This strike did not manage to create links to the growing African-American and Caribbean-American communities in Harlem. One activist did try to organize three Harlem buildings with black tenants but was immediately evicted. As Fogelson notes, participation in rent strikes was "particularly risky" for African-American tenants, who were subject not only to economic pressure but also to the very real threat of violence. Robert M. Fogelson, *The Great Rents Wars: New York, 1917–1929* (New Haven, CT: Yale University Press, 2013), 83.

19   Now the site of a single floor-through apartment that was on sale for $25 million in 2012.

20   "Organize Revolt against High Rents," *New York Times*, March 30, 1920.

Harlem, Brownsville, Borough Park, Tremont, University Heights, and elsewhere. These unions combined into the Greater New York Tenants League, and eventually the Federation of Tenants Organizations of Greater New York.[21] Most of them were deeply inspired by socialist ideals, and often had strong organizational links to the Socialist Party. The East Harlem Tenants League, for example, was based in a local Socialist office. Party politicians like Vladeck, Panken, and Abraham Beckerman promoted the tenant movement as part of their broader political activity. William Karlin, candidate for municipal judge and a former state assemblyman, declared in 1919, "The Socialist Party does not say you should pay less rent. It says you shouldn't pay any rent . . . It is in the Socialist programme that the people shall take the homes and all the land and keep it."[22]

The idea of left-wing parties and labor unions allied with tenants just trying to make ends meet terrified the city's real estate establishment. A member of Mayor John Hylan's Housing Conference Committee declared, "We are approaching a crisis in the housing situation . . . Unless radical action is taken, something drastic will happen."[23] One landlord was deeply alarmed at the formation of what he called a "tenant's soviet" in his building.[24] Tenement owners organized their own groups, including the Federation of Bronx Property Owners

───────────

21   Ibid.

22   Quoted, as a cautionary tale, in "Clarifying Frankness" in the conservative magazine *Harvey's Weekly*, November 1, 1919, 13. See also Fogelson, *The Great Rents Wars*, 86.

23   "Need $560,000,000 for Housing Crisis," *New York Times*, June 17, 1920.

24   Fogelson, *The Great Rents Wars*, 88.

and the Brownsville Landlords Association, to promote their interests and to work with the police to repress tenant activism.[25]

The city and state governments, fearing the potential of the crisis, passed the Emergency Rent Laws, which imposed controls and provided some eviction protections for tenants—the precursor to New York's rent control laws that are still in existence today.

The postwar strikes demonstrated the potential of organized tenant power. But their conclusion also marked one of the housing movement's periodic deaths. Offering protection to a small and dwindling number of households, landlords divided and co-opted the socialist-inspired tenant unions. The unions also fell prey to the reactionary and xenophobic Red Scare that swept the country in the aftermath of the war. Politicians from both mainstream parties attacked the partisan left in New York. Five Socialists—two of whom were also tenant leaders—who had been elected to the New York State Legislature in 1919 were denied their seats, put on trial, and finally expelled in March 1920.

Around the same time, the Socialist Party, divided on the question of joining the Comintern, suffered a schism that led to the emergence of what after 1920 became the Communist Party USA. Both lost influence on housing issues.[26] Many of the connections that they had made between housing and class struggle were lost. Radical housing demands—from public

25   Jared N. Day, *Urban Castles: Tenement Housing and Landlord Activism in New York City, 1890–1943* (New York: Columbia University Press, 1999), 93–118.

26   David A. Shannon, *The Socialist Party of America: A History* (Chicago: Quadrangle, 1955), 126–50.

housing to permanent rent controls based on tenant need—
were dropped. A liberal demand for "fair play" between tenants
and landlords took its place. More conservative tenant leagues
ceased their protest tactics and evolved into professionalized
associations. Their focus became the competent bureaucratic
handling of complaints under the law—a service agency
approach, rather than community organization or movement-
type activity.[27] The Emergency Rent Laws were slowly eroded
and ultimately allowed to lapse.

But during the Great Depression, the housing movement
sprang back to life. This time the movement was more cosmopolitan than in the past, growing beyond the white immigrant
working class. In 1928, the Barbados-born civil rights activist
and Communist Party member Richard B. Moore delivered a
speech that galvanized a meeting of the Washington Heights
Tenant League. Moore's organizing and oratory led to the creation of the Harlem Tenants League, formed to resist what he
described as "the terrible housing conditions imposed upon the
Negro masses under the present oppressive system which is
based upon RENT, INTEREST, and PROFIT."[28]

---

27   Joseph A. Spencer, "New York City Tenant Organizations
and the Post-World War I Housing Crisis," pp. 51–93 in Lawson
and Naison, *The Tenant Movement in New York City*, 88.

28   Richard B. Moore, "Housing and the Negro Masses," pp.
150–2 in *Richard B. Moore, Caribbean Militant in Harlem: Collected
Writings 1920–1972*, ed. W. Burghardt Turner and Joyce Moore
Turner (Bloomington: Indiana University Press, 1988 [1928]), 150.
See also J. Cameron Tudor, "Richard Benjamin Moore: An
Appreciation," *Caribbean Studies* 19.1–2 (1979), 169–74; Naison,
"The Communist Party in Harlem in the Early Depression Years: A
Case Study in the Reinterpretation of American Communism,"
Radical History Review 12 (1976), 68–95.

At the time, Harlem was the site of obvious housing injustices. Many of its tenements, neglected by absentee landlords, were in a state of ruin. And because of widespread discrimination that restricted black tenants to a handful of neighborhoods, rents were high. Many households were composed of recent arrivals from southern US states and the Caribbean who struggled to afford the expensive but dilapidated housing. As Moore put it in an article in the *Daily Worker*,

> The capitalist caste system which segregates Negro workers into Jim Crow districts makes these doubly exploited black workers the special prey of rent gougers. Black and white landlords and real estate agents take advantage of this segregation to squeeze the last nickel out of the Negro working class who are penned into the "black ghetto."[29]

The Harlem Tenants League organized protests to press for rollbacks and necessary repairs. Their efforts ultimately helped win the 1930 passage of laws strengthening the legal position of tenants.

As the Depression hit the city in the early 1930s, housing activism spread throughout the Bronx, Brooklyn, Upper Manhattan, and the Lower East Side. Tenants organized pickets, rallies, and marches and engaged in open warfare with landlords. At a 1932 picket line in what the *New York Times* described as "the Communist quarter of the Bronx," groups of men and women sang the "Internationale." Rioting seemed imminent. The *Times* observed, "The women were the most militant."[30] Protest continued to spread.

---

29   Cited in Mark Naison, *Communists in Harlem during the Depression* (Urbana: University of Illinois Press, 1983), 21.

30   "Rent Strikers Defy Police in Protests," *New York Times*, January 30, 1932, cited in Mark Naison, "From Eviction Resistance

Throughout the city, activists blocked evictions by barricading apartments, harassing marshals, and disrupting movers. Neighbors found space in their already cramped apartments to accommodate families facing homelessness because of their actions. At night they guarded the furniture of evictees, or moved it back inside.

Landlords too became better organized, establishing funds to help each other meet bill payments when their tenants were on strike, circulating blacklists of politically active tenants, and arranging for the police and city marshals to attack picket lines with the goal of "taking the streets away from the strikers."[31]

As the Depression ground on and then war began, government relief efforts provided assistance to some. But many communities remained desperate.

Working-class tenants were not the only ones suffering during the Depression. In 1933, homeowners in Sunnyside Gardens in Queens, New York, organized a strike in support of debt restructuring and against foreclosure.[32] Middle-class activists led rent strikes in 1934 in Sugar Hill, an affluent section of Harlem, and organized protests in the Lower East Side's limited-dividend development Knickerbocker Village. In 1936, tenant activists from across New York formed the City-Wide Tenants League. Headed by Heinz Norden, a writer and translator of Goethe and Rilke who "represented the quintessential 'Popular

---

to Rent Control: Tenant Activism in the Great Depression," pp. 94–133 in Lawson and Naison, *The Tenant Movement in New York City*, 104.

31   Naison, "From Eviction Resistance to Rent Control," 110.

32   Daniel Pearlstein, "Sweeping Six Percent Philanthropy Away: The New Deal in Sunnyside Gardens," *Journal of Planning History* 9.3 (2010), 170–82.

Front personality',"[33] City-Wide became a bridge between liberals and radicals of various stripes and classes. Working with other grassroots campaigns as well as with lawmakers, City-Wide engaged in a style of organizing that represented "a shrewd combination of mass protest tactics and legal representation,"[34] which proved highly effective.

As with previous mobilizations, the housing movements in the 1930s and 1940s drew strength from leftist political parties. The American Labor Party (ALP)—created by Lower East Side garment workers seeking a way outside the Democratic Party to support Roosevelt and La Guardia—placed tenant politics at the center of their electoral strategy. ALP members like Vito Marcantonio, the immensely popular US representative and City Council member from East Harlem, and Mike Quill, a former Irish republican and communist sympathizer who headed the city's powerful Transport Workers Union, were steadfast supporters of tenant's rights.[35]

The Communist Party was also a major instigator of strikes and anti-eviction actions. Tenants were consistently supported by the two Communist members of the City Council, Peter Cacchione, an Italian-American from Brooklyn, and Benjamin Davis, an African-American from Harlem.[36] But the historian

---

33   Naison, "From Eviction Resistance to Rent Control," 119. Norden, dismissed from his job due to his communist associations, eventually settled outside the US permanently and became associated with radical and antiwar circles in London.

34   Ibid., 123. See also Joel Schwartz, *The New York Approach: Robert Moses, Urban Liberals, and Redevelopment of the Inner City* (Columbus: Ohio State University Press, 1993), 46–8.

35   Gold, *When Tenants Claimed the City*, 19.

36   Ibid. Davis would later be kicked out of the City Council and imprisoned on charges of conspiracy to overthrow the US government, stemming from his Communist Party membership.

Mark Naison notes that the Communists lacked legitimacy as well as overall strategy. "The Party had no systematic analysis of housing issues and no legislative solution to the housing crisis."[37] They acted as much out of a desire to increase party membership as out of solidarity with the suffering of working-class households. Nonetheless, Communist-led Unemployed Councils and communist residents of the Bronx co-ops provided significant support for many actions.

Tenant radicals did not succeed in revolutionizing the housing system, as some wished. Yet they did help create the conditions in which concrete gains were won. Throughout the 1930s and 1940s, a series of laws and court decisions helped establish a new system of tenant rights in the city, including rules about rent increases, building maintenance, and the right to picket. Two of the central pieces of New York's housing system— public housing and rent control—were first created in this period. And numerous smaller-scale settlements with individual landlords won rollbacks and other concessions for tenants across the city. These victories were all compromises, reflecting the needs of the urban growth machine as much as those of the housing movement.[38] But without the decades of pressure from tenants, New York's housing miseries would certainly have been worse.

---

37 Ibid., 106.

38 On the concept of the growth machine, see John R. Logan and Harvey L. Molotch, *Urban Fortunes: The Political Economy of Place*, new ed. (Berkeley, CA: University of California Press, 2007 [1987]).

Housing Movements of the Postwar Metropolis

By the end of World War II, New York's housing movements had entered a new phase. Thanks to the New Deal, wartime interventionism, and the growing consensus in support of slum clearance, the state was increasingly active in all corners of the housing system.

As the historian Roberta Gold notes, the designs of urban redevelopment technocrats like Robert Moses and the leaders of the Regional Plan Association "aligned with the logic of capital as much as with the fastidiousness of the planning gentry."[39] Urban renewal represented the exercise of state power largely in order to further the goals of the real estate industry. Throughout the 1940s and 1950s, activists geared up to fight it.

The housing movements of New York's triumphant postwar era therefore faced a wider array of targets than before: private landlords and their continued squeeze on tenants, but also the state itself. Protesters targeted the failure of government policy to regulate private housing and provide adequate numbers of public housing units. But they also targeted the destruction of working-class communities brought about by urban renewal itself. Activists knew there was no contradiction in these positions, despite the slum clearance establishment telling them that to oppose redevelopment was to oppose housing progress.

Tenant leagues based in New York City Housing Authority (NYCHA) public housing developments provided some of the most cohesive movement organizations in this period. When NYCHA began a drive to evict families whose incomes had risen over a previously set ceiling, a new group, the Inter-project Tenants Council, was organized to block evictions. Some

---

39   Gold, *When Tenants Claimed the City*, 43.

NYCHA tenant and resident leagues developed into formidable local power blocs, such as those in Williamsburg Houses, Red Hook Houses, and the massive and well-organized Queensbridge Houses. But NYCHA residential activism was undermined by rules prohibiting the use of community facilities for "political" purposes and by the broader climate of anti-radical suspicion. Public housing in New York and other cities was suspected of being a nest of subversives. And as the urban renewal leviathan continued to grow in strength, the objections of some of its supposed beneficiaries sounded hollow. The public housing resident leagues began "steadily losing moral influence."[40]

Other groups contesting urban renewal and slum clearance faced similar challenges. The fight over the development of Stuyvesant Town and Peter Cooper Village, which began in 1943, typified such conflicts. The project, an early public–private partnership between the La Guardia administration and the Metropolitan Life Insurance Company, threatened to displace 3,800 working-class families. Its architecture and site design strongly resembled early public housing developments, right down to its whites-only resident selection policy. The United Tenants League of Greater New York, a coalition of radical tenants, joined with liberals from the United Neighborhood Houses and other groups to oppose the plan. But an alliance of liberal housing groups, real estate interests, and members of the city government convinced the tenants that cooperating with the growth machine was their best hope, and the project's opposition waned.[41]

---

40   Joel Schwartz, "Tenant Power in the Liberal City, 1943–1971," pp. 134–208 in Lawson and Naison, *The Tenant Movement in New York City*, 149.

41   Ibid., 138–9.

Despite numerous setbacks, and the difficulty of going up against urban renewal operators like Moses and his associates, most neighborhoods on the urban renewal chopping block manifested some form of protest. Save Our Homes committees were organized in neighborhoods throughout the city. Some of these efforts were aided by charities like the Community Service Society and by settlement houses, which had been solid supporters of slum clearance but by the late 1950s were becoming more involved with tenant politics. Tenant activists opposed to urban renewal also garnered support from urbanists like Lewis Mumford, Charles Abrams, and Jane Jacobs, who in addition to writing a famous critique of Moses was also a tireless neighborhood activist in Greenwich Village.[42] Slowly, neighborhood campaigns throughout the five boroughs turned public opinion and the political establishment against urban renewal.

One of New York's most enduring housing organizations, the Metropolitan Council on Housing, dates from this period.[43] Founded in 1959, Met Council brought together tenants, labor organizers, neighborhood leaders, American Labor Party and Communist Party radicals, and professionals from middle- and working-class backgrounds. It drew on the talent and experience of stalwart activists like Frances Goldin, Jane and Robert Wood, Bill Stanley, Esther Rand, and Jane Benedict. Working

---

42   Thanks to the success of *The Death and Life of Great American Cities* (New York: Vintage, 1961), Jacobs became prominent as an opponent of urban renewal. But as is apparent from Lawson, Gold, Schwartz, and other historians, the narrative that currently dominates our understanding of urban renewal politics— the epic battle between Jacobs and Moses—oversimplifies this complex period.

43   Ibid., 165–72.

the courts, the streets, and the media, Met Council in the early 1960s organized campaigns to demand public housing, protest neighborhood destruction, and propose alternative plans for neighborhoods including the Upper West Side, Yorkville, Chelsea, and elsewhere. Met Council would quickly become "one of the most effective tenant groups in the nation,"[44] and a pillar of New York's housing movement. Through the 1960s, it remained tied to its Old Left roots.

Meanwhile, a new wave of housing protest was gathering force. Jesse Gray was a military veteran and Communist Party member who in his younger days had studied the Glasgow rent strikes and *The Housing Question*.[45] He began organizing African-American tenants in Harlem in the mid-1950s. Despite some state efforts at amelioration, Harlem's housing crisis had been ongoing for decades. In response, Gray's organization, the Lower Harlem Tenants Council, soon renamed the Community Council on Housing (CCH), organized tenant associations, block captains, rallies, marches, and strikes.

Throughout the 1950s, the Tenants Council's efforts did little to alter the area's living conditions. But by the early 1960s,

---

44   Peter Dreier, "The Tenant's Movement in the United States," 268.

45   Gold, *When Tenants Claimed the City*, 113–45. On Jesse Gray and CCH more generally, see Mandi Isaacs Jackson, "Harlem's Rent Strike and Rat War: Representation, Housing Access and Tenant Resistance in New York, 1958–1964," *American Studies* 47.1 (2006), 53–79; Joel Schwartz, "The New York City Rent Strikes of 1963–1964," *Social Service Review* 57.4 (1983), 545–64; Michael Lipsky, *Protest and City Politics: Rent Strikes, Housing and the Power of the Poor* (Chicago: Rand McNally, 1970); "Harlem Slum Fighter Jesse Gray," *New York Times*, December 31, 1963.

drawing strength from the civil rights movement, Harlem's residents, and tenants in other communities of color, reenergized the housing movement.

CCH's most famous moment occurred on December 30, 1963. Five tenants who lived in tenements on 117th Street were in court over their non-payment of rent. In front of an eager crowd of supporters and the press, they introduced outrageous evidence of their inhumane housing conditions: three large, dead rats.

The dead rodents were not admissible as evidence in court. But the judge did endorse the right to withhold rent in hazardous conditions.[46] The rat stunt, a media event skillfully coordinated by Gray, succeeded in attracting the city's attention to conditions in Harlem. CCH continued to press their campaign. The Harlem rent strikes would continue for two years.

A number of observers questioned Gray's penchant for publicity as well as his strategy, which ended up embroiling tenants in the court system.[47] But CCH's direct actions contributed to a number of improvements: large-scale housing inspections in Harlem, increased scrutiny of shady landlords, priority for rent strikers' admission to NYCHA buildings, and new

---

46   Samuel Kaplan, "Slum Rent Strike Upheld by Judge," *New York Times*, December 31, 1963. Judge Ribaudo's decision differed from the subsequent Moritt decision in that the former ordered the tenants to pay their rent to the court, which would pay the landlord when repairs had been carried out—whereas Moritt allowed that tenants did not need to pay any rent at all.

47   E.g., Schwartz, "New York City Rent Strikes"; Frances Fox Piven and Richard A. Cloward, "Rent Strike: Disrupting the System," *New Republic*, December 2, 1967, 11–15.

public awareness of racial discrimination by the city housing apparatus.[48] As protests spread, housing bureaucrats who had been pushing for reform could use the public pressure to strengthen their cases within their agencies.[49]

Harlem's rent uprising was mirrored elsewhere in the city. Mobilization for Youth, an organization coordinated by the academics Frances Fox Piven and Richard Cloward, stepped up their work with tenants on the Lower East Side, forming a rent strike committee that included Jesse Gray, Met Council, Puertorriqueños Unidos, and the University Settlement. The radical Brooklyn chapter of the Congress of Racial Equality (CORE), a national civil rights organization, began supporting rent strikes in Bedford-Stuyvesant. Elsewhere in Brooklyn, tenants in Red Hook ceased making payments on their uninhabitable apartments. This led to a court ruling that landlord refusal to make necessary repairs constituted wrongful eviction—and thus tenants were entitled to live rent-free until the situation was remedied. The judge, Fred Moritt, later said, "I am merely applying the ancient and elementary law that you don't owe for what you don't get. That is true whether it's Park Avenue, Brooklyn or Park Avenue, New York."[50]

The tenant movement and the growing civil rights movement in the city amplified each other. The NAACP and other prominent civil rights organizations publicly aligned with rent

---

48   Fritz Umbach, *The Last Neighborhood Cops: The Rise and Fall of Community Policing in New York Public Housing* (Piscataway, NJ: Rutgers University Press, 2011), 72; Jackson, "Harlem's Rent Strike and Rat War."

49   Gold, *When Tenants Claimed the City*, 125.

50   Charles Grutzner, "Court Halts Rent for 'Unfit' Slums," *New York Times*, January 9, 1964.

strikers in Harlem. CORE became more involved, declaring the housing problem to be one of the main reasons for their traffic "stall-in" outside the 1964 World's Fair.[51]

Housing activism was also drawing support from the emerging language and tactics of Black Power. At a rally against police brutality in Harlem in the summer of 1964, Jesse Gray, increasingly aligned with Malcolm X, called for "guerrilla warfare."[52] Housing was part of the ten-point program of the Black Panther Party, which organized rent strikes, community health clinics, and protests in Harlem, the Bronx, and Brooklyn. The Panthers' comrades in the Puerto Rican community, the Young Lords Party, joined them in mobilizing around housing, health, and city services.

As the 1970s began, housing insurrection was once again gripping the city. On the Upper West Side, activists moved working-class black and Latino families into buildings that had been emptied for urban renewal.[53] Named Operation Move-In, the squatters' movement soon spread to Morningside Heights, Chelsea, and the Lower East Side. I Wor Kuen, a Chinatown youth organization modeled on the Young Lords and the Panthers, led a community health campaign and squatted a downtown building owned by the Bell Telephone Company.[54]

---

51   Craig Turnbull, "'Please Make No Demonstrations Tomorrow': The Brooklyn Congress of Racial Equality and Symbolic Protest at the 1964–65 World's Fair," *Australasian Journal of American Studies* 17.1 (1998), 22–41.

52   Junius Griffin, "'Guerrilla War' Urged in Harlem," *New York Times*, July 20, 1964.

53   David K. Shipler, "Poor Families Taking Over Condemned Buildings," *New York Times*, April 24, 1970.

54   Gold, *When Tenants Claimed the City*, 192.

The 1960s and early 1970s saw the biggest wave of the housing movement since World War II. Building from radical currents stirred by civil rights and Black Power, and bridging the Old and New Left, activists successfully linked the housing question to larger struggles surrounding racism, class, and inequality.

But historians like Joel Schwartz see the era as a failure: "tenants were no more able to deter footloose landlords than labor unions were able to deter footloose industrial employers . . . In the end, it was hundreds of thousands of low-income tenants who found themselves out in the cold."[55] After the 1960s, residential abandonment became endemic. Public housing and rent control would never again expand. The fiscal crisis of the 1970s would trigger renewed residential misery in the city as well as a right turn politically. Not only did activists fail to transform the housing system; the infrastructure of reform was bent further towards the interests of real estate.

Housing Movements in Neoliberal New York

The 1970s marked a turning point in the city's housing history. Until then, activists seeking to improve and democratize housing were on the offensive. They faced many powerful opponents and suffered many defeats, but the prospect of changing the housing system through serious social and political intervention still seemed plausible. After that point, the city's post-1970s activists continued to fight difficult battles in unfriendly conditions, but were largely limited to defensive actions.

In the decades following the mid-1970s fiscal crisis, New

---

55   Schwartz, "Tenant Power in the Liberal City," 196–7.

York underwent a regime change. The city's social democratic polity, limited and contradictory as it was, yielded to a neoliberal growth model.[56] At first, under the mayoral administrations of Abe Beame and Ed Koch, this process took the form of cutbacks and privatization. Later, under Rudolph Giuliani, more aggressive social policies were rolled out.[57] The whole process was propelled by, and in turn contributed to, an epochal change in the city's economy. New York had been experiencing industrial job loss for two decades since manufacturing's peak in 1950. But by the 1970s, deindustrialization was wreaking havoc on the city's working-class neighborhoods. At the same time, the finance, insurance, and real estate sectors expanded.

The neoliberal transformation of the city initially spurred two trends in housing: gentrification and abandonment. These processes seemed to be polar opposites, but critical observers recognized them as two sides of the same coin.[58] Both were

56 Joshua B. Freeman, *Working Class New York: Life and Labor since World War II* (New York: New Press, 2000), 55–71; Kim Moody, *From Welfare State to Real Estate: Regime Change in New York City, 1974 to the Present* (New York: New Press, 2007); David J. Madden, "Urbanism in Pieces: Publics and Power in Urban Development," PhD dissertation, Columbia University (2010), 3–8; Robert Fitch, *The Assassination of New York* (New York: Verso, 1973).

57 See Jamie Peck and Adam Tickell, "Neoliberalizing Space," pp. 33–57 in Neil Brenner and Nik Theodore, eds, *Spaces of Neoliberalism: Urban Restructuring in North America and Western Europe* (Malden, MA: Blackwell, 2002).

58 Peter Marcuse, "Gentrification, Abandonment and Displacement: Connections, Causes and Policy Responses in New York City," *Journal of Urban and Contemporary Law* 28 (1985), 196–240.

consequences of the commodification of housing in the context of rapid urban economic change. Both were exacerbated by government policy.[59] And both became targets for housing activists.

Abandonment brought waves of destruction to New York neighborhoods. When landlords decided that maintaining their buildings was no longer profitable, many simply walked away from them. Some, seeking insurance payouts, also set their buildings on fire—with or without tenants inside. As poor New Yorkers faced increased joblessness and impoverishment, the rate of abandonment exploded. There were approximately 1,000 abandoned buildings in 1961, a figure that increased to about 7,000 in 1968. For most of the 1970s, the city lost nearly 40,000 units per year.[60] Into the 1980s, the combination of abandonment, arson, service cuts, and eventually the AIDS epidemic led to deadly and mutually reinforcing housing and health disasters.[61]

---

59   See Tom Angotti, *New York for Sale: Community Planning Confronts Global Real Estate* (Cambridge, MA: MIT Press, 2008), 77; Neil Smith, *The New Urban Frontier: Gentrification and the Revanchist City* (New York: Routledge, 1996), 22–4.

60   Frank P. Braconi, "In Re *In Rem*: Innovation and Expediency in New York's Housing Policy," pp. 93–118 in Michael H. Schill, ed., *Housing and Community Development in New York City: Facing the Future* (Albany, NY: SUNY Press, 1999), 94.

61   Rodrick Wallace and Deborah Wallace, *A Plague on Your Houses: How New York Was Burned Down and National Public Health Crumbled* (New York: Verso, 1998); Rodrick Wallace and Deborah Wallace, "Origins of Public Health Collapse in New York City: The Dynamics of Planned Shrinkage, Contagious Urban Decay and Social Disintegration," *Bulletin of the New York Academy of Medicine* 66.5 (1990), 391–434.

The activists' response to this catastrophe was to take matters into their own hands. Groups like Los Sures in Williamsburg and Banana Kelly in Longwood helped tenants take direct control of abandoned properties and turn them into cooperatives. Some of these efforts began with successful rent strikes. Landlords simply quit, leaving well-organized tenants with months' worth of withheld rent that they invested in fixing their buildings themselves. In other cases, homesteaders moved into emptied shells with the explicit intent to rehabilitate them through sweat equity.[62]

Many buildings that were abandoned by landlords became government property. Through the legal procedure of *in rem* acquisition, the city could take ownership of properties in tax arrears. By 1979 the city owned 40,000 occupied and 60,000 empty apartments.[63] The New York City Department of Housing Preservation and Development became, after the New York City Housing Authority, the second-biggest landlord in New York. The city's huge stock of *in rem* properties allowed it to expand the supply of low-income housing. But with a government unwilling and unprepared to take advantage of the crisis to transform its housing system in a deeper way, *in rem* "became an

---

62   Nicole Marwell, *Bargaining for Brooklyn: Community Organizations in the Entrepreneurial City* (Chicago: The University of Chicago Press, 2007), 44–51; Paul S. Grogan, "Proof Positive: A Community-Based Solution to America's Affordable Housing Crisis," *Stanford Law and Policy Review* 7.2 (1996), 159–71; Jacqueline Leavitt and Susan Saegert, "The Community-Household: Responding to Housing Abandonment in New York City," *Journal of the American Planning Association* 54.4 (1988), 489–500.

63   Braconi, "In Re *In Rem*," 98. This growth was partly a result of a new law that came into effect in 1977 making the *in rem* process easier.

expensive symbol of all that New York's progressive housing tradition had sought to avoid."[64] In some areas, the city proved to be just as careless as the worst rent gouger. In other parts of town, the city used its *in rem* properties, as well as tax subsidies like J-51 and 421-a, as the building blocks for state-led gentrification.[65]

At the same time as abandonment was destroying some neighborhoods, gentrification was displacing poor residents from others. Anti-gentrification activism tended to be locally based and fractured. But from the beginnings of large-scale gentrification in the city in the 1970s and 1980s, groups objected loudly to displacement, commodification, and profiteering, and proposed alternatives.

On the Lower East Side, speculators were pursuing the well-worn strategy of buying occupied tenements, forcing out rent-regulated tenants, and raising the rent. The city wanted to use its substantial stock of buildings acquired through *in rem* to hasten the area's redevelopment. In response, housing groups like the Cooper Square Community Development Committee and Good Ole Lower East Side (GOLES) joined churches, settlement houses, social service providers, and others to form the Lower East Side Joint Planning Council (JPC).[66] Having

---

64   Ibid., 94.

65   William Sites, *Remaking New York: Primitive Globalization and the Politics of Urban Community* (Minneapolis, MN: University of Minnesota Press, 2003), 69–100; Ronald Lawson with Reuben B. Johnson III, "Tenant Responses to the Urban Housing Crisis, 1970–1984," 209–71 in Lawson and Naison, *The Tenant Movement in New York City*, 239–42, 247–51.

66   Sites, *Remaking New York*, 110–19; Christopher Mele, *Selling the Lower East Side: Culture, Real Estate, and Resistance in New York City* (Minneapolis, MN: University of Minnesota Press, 2000), 258–62.

seen how the redevelopment process had turned once-industrial SoHo into an exclusive enclave, the JPC put forward a series of plans to stem speculation in the neighborhood, including public housing but focusing on affordable cooperatives. Nonetheless, the city pushed forward with the plan to privatize its holdings in the area. Despite some token concessions to the JPC, evictions, rent increases, and conversions became everyday occurrences on the Lower East Side.

This pattern was repeated throughout the city. Plans were often proposed at the community level and then disregarded by the city.[67] Anti-gentrification activists were not the irrational refuse-niks that their critics made them out to be. They offered their own visions of what their neighborhoods should become. But especially as New York's housing market came roaring back to profitability in the 1980s and 1990s, these alternatives were consistently ignored as real estate interests overpowered neighborhood organizations.

Some of the fiercest opposition on the Lower East Side came from squatters.[68] Growing from its roots in Operation Move-In,

---

67　Even the 1989 city charter revision, which allowed for the community development strategies known as 197a plans, failed to empower tenants and other locals in any serious way. Tom Angotti notes, "the 197a reform was relatively mild and demanded nothing of the city's planning establishment." Angotti, *New York for Sale*, 155.

68　See Clayton Patterson, ed., *Resistance: A Radical Political and Social History of the Lower East Side* (New York: Steven Stories, 2007), 141–260; Hans Pruijt, "Is the Institutionalization of Urban Movements Inevitable? A Comparison of the Opportunities for Sustained Squatting in New York City and Amsterdam," *International Journal of Urban and Regional Research* 27.1 (2003), 141–2; Eric Hirsch and Peter Wood, "Squatting in New York City: Justification and Strategy," *New York University Review of Law and Social Change* 16 (1987–1988), 605–17.

by the 1980s squatting had become a stronger movement. Raids, evictions, power and water stoppages, and battles with the police were common. Groups like the Urban Homestead Assistance Board (UHAB) aided squatters and homesteaders and, when it became necessary, helped them negotiate with the city about the legal status of their homes.

But squatting proved to have serious limitations as a housing strategy. The struggles of squats presented very different problems than those of other oppositional activities. Some squatters voiced concerns that they might be "the real storm troopers of gentrification."[69] Others were essentially individuals acting alone, merely looking to secure housing for themselves with no connection to wider campaigns. And the squatters encountered violent opposition from the city and polarized public opinion regarding their ambiguous approach to property rights.

Squatters, social workers, community organizations, and assorted neighborhood characters all appeared in one of the most notorious moments of the late twentieth-century housing movement: the Tompkins Square Park riot of 1988. The park had become a flashpoint in battles over housing and neighborhood change in downtown Manhattan. In the surrounding streets of the Lower East Side, rising rents and rampant speculation had placed the neighborhood on edge. Anger was particularly focused on one sixteen-story building that abutted Tompkins Square, the Christadora House. Built by a charity in 1929, the building had housed a community center, a welfare office, and a chapter of the Black Panther Party before being boarded up and auctioned to a private bidder in 1978. Making use of a variety of tax breaks and

---

69   Pruijt, "Is the Institutionalization of Urban Movements Inevitable?," 148.

subsidies, Citibank backed its conversion into luxury condominiums in 1984. The appearance of conspicuous wealth in a sea of poverty made the building an icon of the new housing inequality. One resident writer said that local activists regarded the building as "Satan incarnate."[70]

By the summer of 1988, the New York City Police Department had already sought to enforce a 1:00 a.m. curfew in the park in response to earlier incidents. On the night of August 6, hundreds of people—squatters, tenants, the homeless, punks, artists, and assorted others—assembled in the square. Armed with firecrackers and boom boxes, chanting "Die Yuppie Scum" while carrying banners declaring "Gentrification Is Class War!" they clashed with more than 400 riot police. Thirty-eight people were injured. The *New York Times* declared, "Class Struggle Erupts Along Avenue B."[71] Eventually more than 100 police brutality complaints were filed.[72]

After the Tompkins Square uprising, it was becoming clear that working-class and poor tenants faced growing pressures. In the 1990s, real estate speculation and cutbacks in government programs led once more to worsening housing crisis. Rents soared, and evictions followed, as building owners tried to get rid of rent-regulated tenants. The numbers of subsidized and rent-stabilized apartments shrank. These trends would continue

---

70   Mark A. Uhlig, "Condominiums Divide Angry Tompkins Square Residents," *New York Times*, August 26, 1988.

71   Michael Wines, "Class Struggle Erupts along Avenue B," *New York Times*, August 10, 1988.

72   Mele, *Selling the Lower East Side*, 263–8; Smith, *The New Urban Frontier*, 4–6; Robert D. McFadden, "Park Curfew Protest Erupts into a Battle and 38 Are Injured," *New York Times*, August 8, 1988.

to the present day. For the non-rich, housing in New York became ever more precarious.[73]

Through the Giuliani and Bloomberg years, the housing landscape became increasingly unaffordable and unequal. Luxury development spread out from its traditional wealthy heartlands to colonize the outer corners of the city. Landlords in "transitional" neighborhoods hired lawyers and thugs to help them kick tenants out of rent-regulated units. Low-income families, especially among the rising numbers of immigrants, spent ever more time working to pay inflated rents, moved farther out from the center, and crammed into ever-smaller spaces.

Rudy Giuliani, the city's mayor from 1994 through 2001, demonized housing activists. Giuliani ordered the eviction of squats and launched a vindictive war against the homelessness and AIDS nonprofit group Housing Works and other housing organizations. His successor, Michael Bloomberg, was less visibly antagonistic. The administration liked to boast that its New Housing Marketplace program had developed or preserved

---

73   Victor Bach and Tom Waters, "Making the Rent: Who's at Risk? Rent-Income Stresses and Housing Hardship among Low-Income New Yorkers" (New York: Community Service Society Update Report, 2008); Tom Waters and Victor Bach, "Closing the Door 2007: The Shape of Subsidized Housing Loss in New York City" (New York: Community Service Society Policy Brief, 2007); Kathe Newman and Elvin K. Wyly, "The Right to Stay Put, Revisited: Gentrification and Resistance to Displacement in New York City," *Urban Studies* 43.1 (2006), 23–57; Jason Hackworth, "Postrecession Gentrification in New York City," *Urban Affairs Review* 37.6 (2002), 815–43; Housing Court Answers, "Eviction Trends," available online at cwtfhc.org; Bruce Lambert, "Higher Stakes in Eviction Battles," *New York Times*, May 8, 2000.

more than 160,000 units of affordable housing. But that program largely assisted middle-class families with incomes well over the poverty line.[74] For Bloomberg, the city was "a luxury product," and he dreamed of luring "a bunch of billionaires around the world to move here."[75] Housing activists and the communities that they represented felt that they had no place in Bloomberg's luxury city.[76]

One of the housing groups that emerged in Bloomberg's New York is the Movement for Justice in El Barrio (MJB). The group was founded by migrants and other low-income residents of East Harlem, taking inspiration both from the direct-action tactics of groups like Take Back the Land and from revolutionary movements like the Zapatistas. MJB organizes against displacement and what they explicitly call "neoliberal gentrification" in this working-class, cosmopolitan neighborhood.[77]

---

74 Association for Neighborhood and Housing Development, "Real Affordability: An Evaluation of the Bloomberg Housing Program and Recommendations to Strengthen Affordable Housing Policy" (New York: ANHD, 2013).

75 Diane Cardwell, "Mayor Says New York Is Worth the Cost," *New York Times*, January 8, 2003; Chris Smith, "In Conversation: Michael Bloomberg," *New York Magazine*, September 7, 2013.

76 Julian Brash, *Bloomberg's New York: Class and Governance in the Luxury City* (Athens, GA: University of Georgia Press, 2011), 110–12.

77 Marianne Maeckelbergh, "Mobilizing to Stay Put: Housing Struggles in New York City," *International Journal of Urban and Regional Research* 36.4 (2012), 655–73; Kara Zugman Dellacioppa, *This Bridge Called Zapatismo: Building Alternative Political Cultures in Mexico City, Los Angeles, and Beyond* (Lanham, MD: Lexington Books, 2009), 152–7.

Their "International Declaration in Defense of El Barrio," published in English and Spanish in March 2008, declares, "the struggle for justice means fighting for the liberation of women, immigrants, lesbians, people of color, gays and the transgender community. We all share a common enemy and it's called neoliberalism."[78] For these activists, the fight over place and displacement in East Harlem links local housing issues to anti-racism, indigenous rights, and a struggle to transform global capitalism:

> This displacement is created by the greed, ambition and violence of a global empire of money that seeks to take total control of all the land, labor and life on earth. Here in El Barrio (East Harlem, New York City), landlords, multi-national corporations and local, state, and federal politicians and institutions want to force upon us their culture of money, they want to displace poor families and rent their apartments to rich people, white people with money . . . They want to displace us to bring in their luxury restaurants, their expensive and large clothing stores, their supermarket chains. They want to change our neighborhood. They want to change our culture. They want to change that which makes us Latino, African-American, Asian and Indigenous. They want to change everything that makes us El Barrio.[79]

MJB's declaration was issued in response to the $225 million purchase of forty-seven buildings in East Harlem by Dawnay

---

78 Movement for Justice in El Barrio, "International Declaration in Defense of El Barrio," March 2, 2008, available online at Leftturn.org.

79 Ibid.

Day, a London-based property and financial services company. Dawnay Day executives were famous for their penchant for yachts, art collecting—and tenant harassment.[80] According to activists, the company shut off power and heat, charged for basic repairs, and allowed rats and vermin to spread, all in an effort to chase out longtime rent-regulated residents and replace them with a more lucrative class of tenant. Its director had publicly vowed "to bring along Harlem's gentrification."[81] MJB, along with Community Voices Heard (CVH) and other housing groups, became a crucial lifeline for residents after Dawnay Day went bust, leaving their buildings in legal and administrative limbo.

Throughout the Bloomberg era, in a manner reminiscent of the movement against urban renewal, neighborhoods across the city organized against displacement, megaprojects, and luxury housing. Opposition to the inequality of the Bloomberg years was one of the inspirations for Occupy Wall Street, which began their encampment in Zuccotti Park on September 17, 2011. The movement's largest housing protest took place a few months later, when a faction called Occupy Our Homes led a march and began a small occupation of foreclosed homes in Brooklyn. Activists associated with the Occupy movement led a grassroots response to Hurricane Sandy in 2012, distributing aid to low-income households throughout the areas damaged by the storm. But since then, the housing branch of the Occupy movement has, like many residential movements that preceded it, has seemingly gone into remission.

---

80   Christine Haughney, "Tenants Struggle as British Landlord Goes Bust," *New York Times*, December 21, 2009.

81   Michael Gould-Wartofsky, "El Barrio Fights Back against Globalized Gentrification," *Counterpunch*, April 22, 2008.

Mayor Bill de Blasio, who took office on January 1, 2014, has closer ties to housing activists than any mayor since La Guardia. His policies and appointments have clearly made a difference in some cases. A handful of projects have been forced to include more affordable units than originally planned and required to keep them "affordable" for longer. And his administration has prohibited what housing activists christened "poor doors"—separate entrances to the "affordable" spaces in the otherwise luxury apartment buildings that are built with valuable height bonuses offered by the city in exchange for including the below-market units.

But compared to the resources and space consumed by luxury housing, these changes seem insignificant. Many housing activists see the de Blasio administration's strategy as "too little, too late."[82] Others see his policies as essentially a continuation of those of Bloomberg.[83] And even if the mayor himself asserted a harder line, the city's housing policy is a complex contraption that resists change.

The Rent Guidelines Board's rent freeze vote is a case in point. The mayor's appointees listened to tenant activists and voted not to increase rents on one-year leases. But the freeze did not extend to two-year leases as tenants had demanded, and little action was taken to help tenants on other important issues tied to the debate. Compared to the Giuliani or Bloomberg years, the climate in New York today is more amenable to

---

82   Steven Wishnia, "De Blasio's Housing Plan: Too Little, Too Late?," *Tenant/Inquilino*, May 2014.

83   Real Affordability for All, "A Tale of One Housing Plan: How Bill de Blasio's New York Is Abandoning the Same Low-Income Voters Left Behind during the Bloomberg Years" (New York: Real Affordability for All, 2016); Samuel Stein, "De Blasio's Doomed Housing Plan," *Jacobin* 15–16 (2014), 11–17.

housing activism. Yet the vast political and economic structures of the city are still organized in favor of elite interests. The protections that earlier housing movements won in order to insulate households from the violence of the market are being steadily stripped away. Rent regulation is being undermined. Public housing is in a critically under-maintained condition. Activists are working hard just to keep public housing and rent control around—their expansion seems a distant prospect.

In some ways, housing activism in New York today has much continuity with the past. Veteran organizations like the Metropolitan Council, Tenants & Neighbors, the Pratt Area Community Council, and UHAB continue to have a major presence in the city. Neighborhood-based grassroots organizations are still active in campaigns against displacement and for affordability, access, and safety, including groups like MJB, GOLES, CVH, the Committee against Anti-Asian Violence, and Families United for Racial and Economic Equality. The city is still home to well-organized tenant unions in Crown Heights, Chinatown, Flatbush, and elsewhere, as well as in NYCHA developments in all five boroughs. Following in the footsteps of groups like City-Wide, housing groups today operate in alliances including the Alliance for Tenant Power, the Right to the City Alliance, and Real Affordability for All. And as in the past, contemporary activists have strong allies in the philanthropic sector, including the Community Service Society and the Legal Aid Society.

As well, housing activists continue to rely on many battle-tested tools. A 2014 protest of two buildings on West 107th Street in Manhattan saw tenants chanting "No rent for rats!"—a phrase used by Jesse Gray decades earlier.[84] In 2010, the Right

---

84   Jan Ransom, "Renters Rat-chet Up Fight," *New York Daily News*, July 2, 2014.

to the City Coalition conducted a count of empty luxury condominiums and proposed appropriating them as housing for low-
income families—an tactic floated during the 1920 housing
battles.[85]

Rent strikes still occur, though they are less frequent than at
high points in mobilization like the late 1910s or mid-1960s. In
recent years, rent strikes have been organized in Fort Greene,
Sunset Park, and elsewhere in the rapidly gentrifying tenements
and row houses of the outer boroughs. Activists have marched
to end landlord subsidies, block evictions, and stop luxury redevelopment plans. They have also taken to the streets to demand
stronger rent control, more effective code enforcement, greater
public safety, more support for public housing, and support for
tenants' rights. These are all long-standing housing movement
objectives.

In other ways, however, contemporary housing activism in
New York is quite different from previous eras. The squatter
movement, for example, has been reduced to a residuum. After
decades of battles, eleven squats were legalized by the Bloomberg
administration in 2002. Other squats became community spaces,
like ABC No Rio, still famous as a social center and host of all-
ages punk matinees. But as the housing market has heated up,
there is a sharply reduced number of vacant buildings available
for squats. As a movement, squatting is no longer a significant
force in housing politics.

And in general, today's movements occur in a neoliberal
context where political possibilities have been constricted.

---

85   New York City Chapter of the Right to the City Alliance,
"People without Homes and Homes without People: A Count of
Vacant Condos in Select NYC Neighborhoods" (New York: Right
to the City Alliance, 2010).

There are few opportunities to debate fundamental issues about the nature of the housing system. Urban politics stays within a narrow consensus. There is little room for movements to assert alternatives within the confines of the contemporary debate.

The housing movements of New York today are struggling against a city that is more unequal and more competitive than at any time since the last Gilded Age. In neoliberal New York, the needs of those who use housing for living are frequently pushed aside. But the city's tenants have been under attack before. It has never been long before they fought back.

For the Housing Struggles Ahead

The history of housing movements in New York shows them involved in a variety of conflicts around many issues, with widely varying results. Neither the identity of the actors nor the means they employ nor their specific goals remain the same. The participants in housing movements may be farmers, or tenants, or immigrants, women, people of color, professionals, homeowners, public housing residents, the elderly, the homeless, punks, students, queer activists, or others, and they are usually some combination of these and more. The means that they employ may be rent strikes, eviction blocking, legislative lobbying, street demonstrations, political mobilization, electoral participation, boycotts, publicity campaigns, squatting, mutual aid, or self-help. Their goals may be fair rent, public housing, security of location, security of tenure, access to financing, integration, opportunities for mobility, or opposition to invasion. What links these disparate actors, actions, and goals is a commitment to one overall project: the defense of housing, which must necessarily take different forms as the nature of the city's housing, politics, and economy changes.

To acknowledge the diversity of housing movement tactics and goals is not to say that they have shown infinite flexibility in their demands. That is not the case, and it is important to acknowledge what housing movements are *not*. Despite what observers assert as the best interest of tenants, housing activists do not march to have their public housing demolished. They do not march to have rent controls removed. They do not march over aesthetics or design issues. They do not demand influxes of more wealthy and powerful neighbors. As a rule, those are outsiders' concerns.

The dominant image of the housing activist is an angry tenant shouting "NO!" Their negativity is said to be their defining factor, such that some mistake popular housing activism with middle-class NIMBYism, which is a different political impulse altogether.

The image of unrelenting negativity is a crude stereotype. But it is true that housing campaigns do at times need to object to plans from developers or the city. In an unequal society, the people who have the means to start projects are the elites. "No" is often the only thing that the relatively powerless are able to say that can be heard by those in power.

Housing activists do in fact have a long history of proposing positive plans. They are frequently told that their ideas are unrealistic because they assert the rights of residents and give insufficient due to economic realities. But refusing to tell the powerful what they want to hear is different than not proposing a plan.

If the history of New York City is any guide, the housing movements of the future will have no choice but to continue these struggles. Decent and accessible housing is not a default condition. Housing must be demanded and protected. Doing so will always combine the positive assertion of the right to housing with the rejection of incursions upon that right. If the inhabitants of New York have learned anything about their dwelling space, it is that they must always be ready to defend it.

Conclusion:

For a Radical Right to Housing

Is housing for everyone a hopelessly utopian goal? Is it plausible to imagine universal and unconditional housing, in sociable and environmentally sustainable communities, as a matter of right rather than a commodified privilege? As an abstract ideal, housing for all is surprisingly common.

The Housing Act of 1949 set out what it saw as the national housing goal of the United States government. The law declared,

> the general welfare and security of the Nation and the health and living standards of its people require housing production and related community development sufficient to remedy the serious housing shortage, the elimination of substandard and other inadequate housing through the clearance of slums and blighted areas, and the realization as soon as feasible of the goal of a decent home and a suitable living environment for every American family . . .[1]

---

1 Committee on Banking and Currency, United States Senate, *Housing Act of 1949: Summary of Provision of the National Housing Act of 1949* (Washington, DC: Government Printing Office, 1949), 1.

The 1949 Act, including its objective of "a decent home and a suitable living environment for every American family," passed with bipartisan support. And Congress reaffirmed its basic principles on numerous subsequent occasions.

New York State has its own distinctive constitutional approach to housing rights. New York's Constitution declares that the "aid, care and support of the needy are public concerns and shall be provided by the state."[2] *Callahan v. Carey*, a 1979 lawsuit filed on behalf of six homeless men living on the Bowery, put this line to the test. *Callahan* ended in a consent decree establishing a legally enforceable constitutional right to shelter.[3]

In fact, formulations about a right to housing or shelter are far more widespread than many realize. Language acknowledging the responsibility of states to supply adequate housing for their citizenry appears in the national constitutions of sixty-nine countries.[4] And such a right has long been promoted by the United Nations General Assembly and other major

---

2   New York Constitution, Article XVII, § 1.

3   This right is interpreted as requiring New York State to provide emergency housing for homeless people—a right which is important for the homeless and their legal advocates, even if it does not correspond to universal access to high-quality or even decent housing. See Bradley R. Haywood, "The Right to Shelter as a Fundamental Interest under the New York State Constitution," *Columbia Human Rights Law Review* 34 (2002), 157–96; Christine Robitscher Ladd, "A Right to Shelter for the Homeless in New York State," *New York University Law Review* 61 (1986), 272–99.

4   United Nations Housing Rights Programme, *Housing Rights Legislation: Review of International and National Legal Instruments*, UN Human Settlement Programme Report No. 1 (Nairobi: Office of the High Commissioner of Human Rights, 2002), 37.

international organizations. A right to housing was enshrined in Article 25 of the Universal Declaration of Human Rights adopted in 1948 and in numerous other widely adopted treaties.[5]

The goal of universal housing, then, is not some sectarian fantasy. It is in fact widely held. Nearly all political actors and parties claim to support some version of it.[6] But there is a contradiction between the end of housing for all and the means that are supposed to accomplish it: market systems and capitalist states. Ideological visions about benevolent government policy or efficient markets hide this essential conflict.

On its own, the mere idea of universal access to good housing is not a challenge to the existing political-economic order but a perpetually deferred promise that the system uses to legitimize itself. Merely declaring a universal right to housing is not the same as actually providing housing for all. Perhaps that is one reason why such rights can be so widely acclaimed.

A right to housing is no panacea. There is no single legal formula that, on its own, can bring an end to the ongoing housing crisis. As with all rights, everything depends on how it

---

5   Office of the United Nations High Commissioner for Human Rights, and UN HABITAT, "The Right to Adequate Housing," Fact Sheet no. 21 rev. 1 (Geneva: United Nations, n.d.), 11.

6   Very few opponents of universal housing provision are willing publicly to follow their reasoning to its logical conclusion: that the threat of homelessness is needed to enforce the imperative to labor. In the words of conservative legal scholar Robert Ellickson, "advocates [of an unconditional right to housing] have failed to deal with the fundamental fact that a society must maintain incentives to work." Robert C. Ellickson, "The Untenable Case for an Unconditional Right to Shelter," *Harvard Journal of Law and Public Policy* 15.1 (1992), 17.

is interpreted, institutionalized, and enforced. The way forward is to acknowledge the limits of formal rights to housing under the current legal and political system while at the same time pressing for a sufficiently broad, activist conception of those rights. Only with such an approach can a right to housing be used to challenge to residential commodification, alienation, oppression, and inequality today.

Housing as a Right

The language of rights has an ambiguous political track record. Rights can be used for a huge variety of purposes, some of which are emancipatory and some of which are oppressive. Critics link the discourse of rights to imperialism and colonial civilizing projects. Or they see rights as more symbolic than substantive. For some critics, declarations of rights too often amount to ineffective and unenforceable claims, or, even worse, to toothless abstractions that just help unequal societies feel better about their inequality. When the relatively powerless claim rights against the powerful, legal formulas run up against the reality of class hierarchy and domination: "between equal rights force decides."[7] Claims about legal equality, critics argue, only serve to disguise the truth of actual inequality.[8]

---

7   Karl Marx, *Capital: A Critique of Political Economy*, vol. 1, trans. Ben Fowkes (London: Penguin Books, 1976 [1867]), 344.

8   The very concept of rights has obviously been subject to centuries of scholarly and juridical debate, which we are not going to review here. For some recent critical histories, see Samuel Moyn, *The Last Utopia: Human Rights in History* (Cambridge, MA: Harvard University Belknap Press, 2010); Lynn Hunt, *Inventing*

When used in a purely legal sense, rights can function to shore up existing structures and relationships without questioning them. If the right to housing is merely a right to be incorporated into the residential status quo, without changing present methods of distributing the benefits and costs of housing, then it is a weak right indeed. Such a right would remain silent about the social conflicts at the heart of housing politics. The vast bulk of the legal edifice that shapes access to housing exists to protect the rights of property owners. A right to housing that does not challenge and change the current housing system would either be unenforceable or at best end up as a state subsidy for landlords. A legalistic, procedural version of the right to housing is bound to fall short of the results that it promises.

And yet, while arguments criticizing rights should be taken seriously, they are not grounds for dismissing the entire repertoire of rights-based housing politics. The universe of rights is not monolithic. Not all versions of rights end up maintaining the status quo. Under some conditions, rights talk can be a way to demand the impossible. The mere act of trying to claim a right that is unreasonable under the current state of affairs can illustrate the limits of the system and point towards ways to change it.

An actual right to housing necessarily implies fundamental challenges to the existing system. The efficacy of this sort of right is that it can articulate a demand around which a mass movement can

---

Human Rights: A History (New York: Norton, 2007); Wendy Brown, "'The Most We Can Hope For . . .': Human Rights and the Politics of Fatalism," *South Atlantic Quarterly* 103.2 (2004), 451–63; Duncan M. Kennedy, "The Critique of Rights in Critical Legal Studies," pp. 178–229 in Janet E. Halley and Wendy Brown, eds, *Left Legalism/ Left Critique* (Durham, NC: Duke University Press, 2002).

mobilize: the demand for truly decent housing for all irrespective of one's economic or social status. Across the world, social movements demonstrate that making such a demand can be a route towards housing justice. And in the absence of such rights, housing is abandoned to the political and economic vicissitudes of class society and market provision.

In fact, the pursuit of a right to housing is a strategic objective for activists in many cities. Virtually every major housing protest is suffused with rights talk. Crowds at demonstrations chant, "Fight, fight, fight! Housing is a right!" Banners proclaim, "HOUSING IS A RIGHT NOT A PRIVILEGE." Organizers in the US and abroad draw upon claims about human rights as a viable legal strategy against housing injustice.[9] Opponents of gentrification often end up relying on some version of housing researcher Chester Hartman's idea that there should be a "right to stay put."[10]

A radical right to housing is a special kind of right. It links to the activist conception of rights invoked by the phrase "the right to the city," originally popularized by Henri Lefebvre in 1968 and subsequently made the basis for social movements around

---

9   Joe Hoover, "The Human Right to Housing and Community Empowerment: Home Occupation, Eviction Defence and Community Land Trusts," *Third World Quarterly* 36.6 (2015), 1092–1109; Saki Knafo, "Is Gentrification a Human-Rights Violation?" *The Atlantic*, September 2, 2015; Maria Foscarinis, "Advocating for the Human Right to Housing: Notes from the United States," *New York University Review of Law and Social Change* 30 (2006), 448.

10   Chester Hartman, "The Right to Stay Put," pp. 120–33 in *Between Eminence and Notoriety: Four Decades of Radical Urban Planning* (New Brunswick, NJ: Center for Urban and Policy Research, 2002 [1984]).

the world.[11] From Lefebvre's perspective, the right to the city is a "cry and a demand"; that is, part of social struggle, not an individual legal entitlement.[12] "Right" is not used in its conventional legal sense, but in an ethical and political sense. Lefebvre is not proposing a right to the city as it currently exists, but the right to a transformed city, and the right to transform it. Such a right is not opposed to legally enforceable claims, but it aims at social and political goals that are far broader than that.

A truly radical right to housing must comprise a similarly expansive set of political demands. More than a simple legal claim, a real right to housing needs to take the form of an ongoing effort to democratize and decommodify housing, and to end the alienation that the existing housing system engenders. It would name a set of claims about the housing that everyone in fact deserves, claims legitimized not only by legal mechanisms but also by popular democratic mobilization. It would not be a demand for inclusion within the horizon of housing politics as usual but an effort to move that horizon.

---

11   Henri Lefebvre, "The Right to the City," pp. 63–181 in Eleonore Kofman and Elizabeth Lebas, eds and trans., *Writings on Cities* (Malden, MA: Blackwell, 1996 [1967]). Among the extensive literature on the topic, see Neil Brenner, Peter Marcuse, and Margit Mayer, eds, *Cities for People, Not for Profit: Critical Urban Theory and the Right to the City* (New York: Routledge, 2012); Kafui A. Attoh, "What Kind of Right Is the Right to the City?," *Progress in Human Geography* 35.5 (2011), 669–85; David Harvey, "The Right to the City," *New Left Review* 53 (2008), 23–40; Don Mitchell, *The Right to the City: Social Justice and the Fight for Public Space* (New York: Guildford Press, 2003); Mark Purcell, "Excavating Lefebvre: The Right to the City and Its Urban Politics of the Inhabitant," *GeoJournal* 58 (2002), 99–108; Eugene J. McCann, "Space, Citizenship, and the Right to the City: A Brief Overview," *GeoJournal* 58.2 (2002), 77–9.

12   Lefebvre, "The Right to the City," 158.

People do not only live in homes. They live in neighborhoods and communities. They occupy buildings but also locations in a social fabric. A radical right to housing must affirm and protect this web of relations. It must propose new links between housing and other domains. As Raquel Rolnick, the former UN special rapporteur on housing, argues, "the notion of the human right to adequate housing is not restricted to the access of the house itself . . . the right to housing has to be apprehended in a much broader context."[13] A radical right to housing raises our sights and sees the objective of action more comprehensively, tying together in a common quest broader claims to equality, dignity, solidarity, and welfare.

Transformative Demands

A real right to housing requires fundamental change in the political and economic structures of contemporary society. The housing system is dominated by powerful actors and institutions that have a major interest in maintaining the status quo. And it is deeply shaped by other political and economic spheres with their own structures of inequality and inertia. The state is clearly part of the problem, and yet is absolutely necessary for any solution. What, then, is to be done?

There are better and worse ways to respond to the contradiction between the ideal of housing as a right and the reality of

---

13   Raquel Rolnick, "Place, Inhabitance and Citizenship: The Right to Housing and the Right to the City in the Contemporary Urban World," *International Journal of Urban and Regional Research* 14.3 (2014), 294.

housing in crisis. One bad way is to dispense with the ideal and settle for reforms only at the margins. Even worse is to wait around for some messianic revolution to solve the problem for us, and abandon efforts for change in the meantime.

If housing for all is a commonly held ideal that is impossible under current conditions, the best response is to hold on to the ideal and change current conditions towards realizing a world that more closely resembles it. The way to do this is to formulate demands that are accomplishable in the world as it exists but which point in the direction of deeper change. The right to housing should not be rejected as an unrealizable fantasy but upheld as an object of struggle towards making it a reality.

Not all demands for political and social change are alike.[14] Some reforms, which can be called efficiency reforms, are simply designed to make what is already being done more effective, say by streamlining administrative structures or improving accountability practices. Such reforms are system-maintaining in the obvious sense that they help a given system meet its predetermined goals in a more efficient way.

Other kinds of reform, which we can call liberal reforms, aim at ameliorating the most undesirable aspects of a condition or policy but without addressing their implicit power relations or conflicts of interest. Some of these demands may gesture towards more radical claims, say by highlighting inequality or corporate power, but they do so only incidentally. By quieting dissent without fundamentally changing the political situation, these reforms also often end up being system-maintaining.

---

14 This discussion draws on "Blog #11. Reforms, Radical Reforms, Transformative Claims," *PMarcuse.wordpress.com*, March 25, 2012.

We are interested in what we can identify as transformative demands. They seek to address the systemic causes of inequities and injustices, looking comprehensively at the sources of a particular problem and at the systemic and institutional factors that nurture it. Transformative demands are system-challenging, or what André Gorz calls non-reformist reforms:[15] not attempts to make the current system more resilient, but actions that improve present conditions while also progressively enabling the building of a different world.

Such transformative demands should not, strictly speaking, be seen as utopian. They develop potentials that actually exist at a given level of development, but which are blocked by existing conditions. They are radical, because they seek to address problems not at the surface, but at the root. Such demands that are both actionable and transformative are the best way to respond to the current housing crisis.

---

15   On reformist versus non-reformist or revolutionary reforms, see André Gorz, *Strategy for Labour: A Radical Proposal*, trans. Martin A. Nicolaus and Victoria Ortiz (Boston: Beacon Press, 1967 [1964]). A similar point is made by Nancy Fraser, who differentiates between "affirmative remedies" and "transformative remedies": "By affirmative remedies for injustice I mean remedies aimed at correcting inequitable outcomes of social arrangements without disturbing the underlying framework that generates them. By transformative remedies, in contrast, I mean remedies aimed at correcting inequitable outcomes precisely by restructuring the underlying generative framework." Nancy Fraser, "From Redistribution to Recognition: Dilemmas of Justice in a 'Post-socialist' Age," *New Left Review* 212 (1995), 82. See also Susan S. Fainstein, *The Just City* (Ithaca, NY: Cornell University Press, 2010), 23–56.

Potential Directions

Having concluded that the present situation requires a radical right to housing, what might constitute concrete steps in that direction? We can obviously not offer a set of policies or blueprints. Precise demands need to be tailored to specific conditions and be proposed by local actors. But we can outline directions in which we believe the housing system should move and suggest broad demands that can be posed to the state and other institutions. And we can highlight promising strategies that are being pursued by housing movements across the globe.

Decommodify and de-financialize the housing system. Simply put, prevent housing from being treated as a commodity. This is the overarching goal. Reversing the commodity character of housing must be the core of any answer to the housing crisis. As we have been arguing, the idea that housing should primarily be an asset to accumulate wealth is a product of contemporary legal, economic, and political structures, all of which can be changed. Establishing a real right to housing demands such changes.

There are many routes towards decommodification, even beyond the public provision of housing, which is considered below. These include rent controls, more secure tenancies, public ownership of land, public financing, limits on speculation, and the adoption or re-introduction of regulations on home finance mechanisms. Cities and movements across the world are proposing such restrictions on commodification today. The Right to the City Alliance has promoted the creation of a Community Reinvestment Bank—a public, nonprofit provider of home financing.[16] Laws in

---

16   Right to the City, "Housing and Land: A Need for Transformative Demands," *Transformative Demands Working Paper Series No. 1* (New York: Right to the City, n.d.), 4.

Australia and other countries impose special taxes on ownership by nonresident investors, which could also be banned outright. Cities could institute a land value tax, which recaptures for the public coffers the collectively produced unearned increment from rising land values. A luxury housing tax could at once raise public funds and remove the incentive for the construction of empty luxury investment homes. A foreclosure tax would reduce the number of foreclosures and recoup some of their costs. A tax on empty buildings would reduce land banking by private landlords.

There are other contemporary programs that distribute housing on the basis of need rather than only following market signals. One example is the "Housing First" approach to homelessness used in New York, Los Angeles, and other cities.[17] An application of harm reduction principles that were originally developed in the field of public health, Housing First programs seek to provide the homeless with unconditional, stable housing, going well beyond typical shelters.[18] Such policies do not escape the contradictions of neoliberal social policy, but they do highlight the plausibility of housing provision beyond market logics.[19]

---

17   See Deborah K. Padgett, Leyla Gulcur, and Sam Tsemberis, "Housing First Services for People Who Are Homeless with Co-occurring Serious Mental Illness and Substance Abuse," *Research on Social Work Practice* 16.1 (2006), 74–83; Sam Tsemberis, Leyla Gulcur, and Maria Nakae, "Housing First, Consumer Choice, and Harm Reduction for Homeless Individuals with a Dual Diagnosis," *American Journal of Public Health* 94.4 (2004), 651–6.

18   See Eric Single, "Defining Harm Reduction," *Drug and Alcohol Review* 14.3 (1995), 287–90.

19   See Victoria Stanhope and Kerry Dunn, "The Curious Case of Housing First: The Limits of Evidence Based Policy," *International Journal of Law and Psychiatry* 34 (2011), 275. This particular strategy

The most obvious opportunity for action would be to immediately halt and throw into reverse the processes of deregulation and privatization that are steadily exacerbating the housing crisis. Currently, many governments are actively working to undermine rent control, sell off public residential assets, cut funding for public housing and homeless services, outsource local housing functions, and encourage speculation. If they were interested in staunching the growth of residential suffering, a good starting point for local and national governments would be to immediately refrain from making the problem worse.

Expand, defend, and improve public housing. Public housing is central to any the effective social response to the housing crisis. The strengthening of the existing publicly owned housing stock, and its expansion in new developments, is the only way to simultaneously combat the connected problems of shelter poverty and gentrification. It is the most direct way to ensure that a home can be made available to anyone in need of one. Greatly expanding and improving the residential public sector would be the simplest route to providing a meaningful right to housing for all. For inspiration, we can look to the successful housing programs of the twentieth century, such as that of Red Vienna. The history of public housing in postwar Europe, both east and west, and the huge variation in public housing systems around the world provide plenty of examples of successful models that

---

of exploiting neoliberal contradictions can be seen as a common strategy for harm reduction activists. See Rachel Faulkner-Gurstein, "Getting out of the Ghetto: Harm Reduction, Drug User Health and the Transformation of Social Policy in New York," PhD dissertation, City University of New York Graduate Center, 2015.

could support a viable and popular twenty-first-century public housing sector.[20]

Successfully decommodifying and de-financializing housing requires breaking the monopoly of for-profit developers. Part of the power of private capital in the housing system comes from the fact that the public role has been reduced to facilitating private action. As a result, communities are at the mercy of corporate real estate actors who know that there are currently no alternatives: either they build or no one does. This monopoly of the private sector needs to end.

Supporters of deregulation frequently point out that restrictions on private residential capital would only make the housing problem worse by restricting supply. But that position assumes that the monopoly of the private sector will be maintained for the foreseeable future. This issue would vanish were there a dynamic and permanently nonprofit public system to act as an actual alternative to for-profit development.[21]

Funding for building new public housing should come from general government revenues, so that it does not become dependent upon luxury development, as with inclusionary zoning. New public housing could also be funded by redirecting

---

20   On the wide varieties of contemporary public housing, see Penny Gurstein, Kristin Patten, and Prajna Rao, "The Future of Public Housing: Trends in Public Housing Internationally" (Vancouver, BC: School of Community and Regional Planning, University of British Columbia, 2015); Defend Council Housing, *The Case for Council Housing in 21st Century Britain* (London: Defend Council Housing, 2006).

21   This is one reason why real estate has always been keen to attack public housing and keep its standards as low as possible.

the hundreds of millions of public dollars given away as subsidies to corporate real estate.[22]

Public housing can become a mechanism not only to provide shelter, but also to relieve stress from elsewhere in the housing system. The more public housing is a desirable, accessible, and affordable option, the less scope exists for exploitation by private landlords. Public housing can also help deal with some of the shortcomings of private homeownership. A proposal for a "right to sell" offered by the British geographer Danny Dorling and others would allow private owners in financial distress to sell their homes to local governments and become secure public tenants, avoiding foreclosure while adding to the public housing stock.[23]

But we should not aim to uncritically adopt twentieth-century public housing, which was created in very different conditions than those that prevail in cities today. The residential public sector reflected particular twentieth-century class compromises and political-economic imperatives. It was designed to stabilize the Fordist–Keynesian city: to defuse conflicts, to provide jobs,

---

22 Writing about New York, housing researchers Victor Bach and Tom Waters note that "it is not unusual for the city and the state to make major capital investments in private development. For instance, in 2006 alone, the city committed $254 million to development of the new Yankee and Mets stadiums, along with $325 million in tax exemptions. It is time to make comparable investments in restoring the public housing infrastructure." Victor Bach and Tom Waters, "Strengthening New York City's Public Housing: Directions for Change" (New York: Community Service Society, 2014), 19.

23 Danny Dorling, "The Right to Sell: Towards a National Housing Service?," conference presentation, Housing Privatisation: 30 Years On, University of Leeds, 2010.

to facilitate the work of private developers. This model should not be blindly copied. Public housing should be protected and expanded but also radicalized and democratized. The theorist Alberto Toscano recently argued,

> struggles in public sectors that have already been intensely subjected to forms of managerialism and competitive discipline, when not extensively privatised, will of necessity be inhabited by a contradictory reformism—at once upholding the 'values' embodied in such institutions and subjecting them to critique, asserting the significance of the 'public' as a domain of relative non-commodification while experiencing the parlous effects of governmental control.[24]

Precisely this sort of contradictory, non-reformist reformism is needed now for housing's public sector. What we need is to at once critique, defend, and expand public housing.

This is not to say that private enterprise can have no place in a more just residential system. In a thoroughly transformed and democratized housing system, some form of entrepreneurialism could be a useful tool. But such entrepreneurialism should be at the service of a different, egalitarian housing process and not, as it currently is, the driver of an inegalitarian, profit-focused one.[25]

---

24   Alberto Toscano, "Reforming the Unreformable," pp. 182–9 in Federico Campagna and Emanuele Campiglio, eds, *What We Are Fighting For: A Radical Collective Manifesto* (London: Pluto Press, 2012), 186.

25   Cf. a recent comment by the sociologist Erik Olin Wright, discussing a post-capitalist economy: "There is maybe a space for certain kinds of non-cooperative entrepreneurial individual proprietorships in an economy dominated by socialist relations. I don't

Privilege inhabitants. Make the interests of residents the dominant concern of housing policy. Currently, investors and owners rule the housing system. When conflicts arise, their needs are met and their interests are protected. This must change. The housing system should be reconfigured to privilege the people who live in housing, rather than those who only profit from it.

The general principle of privileging inhabitants ultimately points to the end of private landlordism. But it suggests more immediate steps as well. It means, in the first instance, creating new power relationships between tenants and landlords. To defend vulnerable households, there should be an immediate moratorium on evictions. Renting as well as subletting should be made more secure, as it is in countries like Germany, the Netherlands, Austria, and Belgium.[26] There should be longer or indefinite tenancies, with fewer opportunities for termination or rent increases. There should be additional protections for certain tenants like families or the elderly. This would lessen the opportunities for abuse and diminish the social distinction between forms of tenure.

For households facing foreclosure, there should be public mandates for loan modifications and principal write-downs, possibly using the power of eminent domain, as some have

---

know what the optimal mix of different forms should be." "Why Class Matters," *Jacobin*, December 23, 2015.

26   This is not to romanticize private renting in any of these places—only to point out that more secure tenancies are possible. Kath Scanlon and Ben Kochan, eds, *Towards a Sustainable Private Rented Sector: Lessons from Other Countries* (London: LSE London, 2011).

proposed.[27] Foreclosure is currently a mechanism for dispossession and gentrification, but it could be turned into a force for redistribution of dwelling space in favor of those who inhabit. The Right to the City Alliance proposes tax foreclosure as a way to convert vacant condominiums into publicly owned housing for low-income families.[28] Considering the luxury colonization of much of Manhattan, this may seem unlikely. But it is not out of the question. Paris's city council recently announced a plan to establish a "right of first refusal" for the municipal purchase of properties in gentrifying neighborhoods as an anti-displacement measure.[29]

"Inhabitants" is obviously a heterogeneous category. Plenty of residential disputes stem from the conflicting ways that residents inhabit dwellings. But the basic principle of giving priority to those who live in housing is still a necessary corrective.

Let a thousand housing alternatives bloom. Support wide experimentation in terms of constructing and managing housing. From communes to squats to experimental building techniques and new forms of tenure, the universe of dwelling possibilities is wider and more interesting than it may appear at first. We can learn from these projects.

---

27 Josh Harkinson, "Inside the Radical Plan to Fight Foreclosures with Eminent Domain," *Mother Jones*, January 7, 2013.

28 New York City Chapter of the Right to the City Alliance, "People without Homes and Homes without People: A Count of Vacant Condos in Select NYC Neighborhoods" (New York: Right to the City Alliance, 2010).

29 Feargus O'Sullivan, "Paris Wants to Keep Central Neighborhoods From Becoming 'Ghettos for the Rich,'" *CityLab*, December 19, 2014.

For example, there are many alternative forms of tenure that are currently available in most housing systems: cooperative, mutual, communal, limited-equity co-ownership, and others. All of them depend upon changing the collection of rights, responsibilities, and powers that constitute tenure in the first place. The creation of new forms of tenure should be encouraged.[30]

Again, this is not an unrealistic dream but a concrete reality in communities across the world. Community land trusts are probably the most prominent alternative tenures today. They have their roots in 1960s civil rights organizing against racist land politics in the American South.[31] Different community land trusts vary considerably, but the basic model is that a nonprofit corporation holds land in trust and offers permanently affordable, limited-equity, long-term leases to residents. There are now more than 230 community land trusts in the United States, around 150 in the United Kingdom, and many others elsewhere.[32]

In some instances, alternative forms of neighborhood organization and building techniques have led to encouraging experiments in communal housing. For thirty years, N Street

30 See Peter Marcuse with Richard Clark, "Tenure and the Housing System: The Relationship and the Potential for Change," Working Paper 209-8-4 (Washington: Urban Institute, 1973).

31 James DeFilippis, *Unmaking Goliath: Community Control in the Face of Global Capital* (New York: Routledge, 2004), 92.

32 Tom Moore and Kim McKee, "Empowering Local Communities? An International Review of Community Land Trusts," *Housing Studies* 27.2 (2012), 280–90; David M. Abramowitz, "An Essay on Community Land Trusts: Towards Permanently Affordable Housing," *Mississippi Law Journal* 61 (1991), 663–82.

Cohousing in Davis, California, has been retrofitting a collection of detached homes to create a communal residential space.[33] The recently built LILAC (Low Impact Living Affordable Community) is a group of twenty prefabricated straw-bale houses organized into a co-housing community outside Leeds, England.[34] Freetown Christiania has existed as a large-scale communal squat and major tourist attraction in central Copenhagen since 1971.[35] The twenty-five apartments that make up Berlin's Lebensort Vielfalt (Diverse Living Space) provide housing for a multi-generational group of LGBT residents.[36] Throughout Berlin, there are currently more than three hundred co-housing developments.[37]

We should affirm these initiatives and encourage more of them. They show that actually existing options for housing tenure are already much wider than they often appear. These projects provide access to housing, and represent a creative and communal antidote to residential alienation.

However, there is no guarantee that projects of this sort will constitute truly transformative endeavors. They cannot replace

---

33 Dorit Fromm, "American Cohousing: The First Five Years," *Journal of Architectural and Planning Research* 17.2 (2000), 94–109.

34 "Pioneering Strawbale Housing Project Is a Lesson in Living," *Yorkshire Post*, April 4, 2015.

35 Alessandro Coppola and Alberto Vanolo, "Normalising Autonomous Spaces: Ongoing Transformations in Christiania, Copenhagen," *Urban Studies* 52.6 (2015), 1152–68.

36 Kate Connolly, "LGBT Housing Project Unites Generations out in Berlin," *The Guardian*, October 28, 2012.

37 See Melissa Fernández Arrigoitia and Kathleen Scanlon, "Co-designing Senior Co-housing," *Urban Design* 136 (2015), 28–30.

public investment in housing. They can too easily become the exclusive domain of affluent households, and they are liable to be reintegrated into the logic of commodification. To avoid this, experiments in alternative tenure should be connected as much as possible to larger-scale efforts, to marginalized groups and to public housing authorities, so that they avoid being interesting exceptions to an otherwise unchanged residential condition.

Democratize housing management. Make housing management more democratic and community-based. Housing movements have long made residents' control of their dwellings one of their central demands.[38] That tenants especially lack control of their homes is one of the causes of residential alienation. In order to disalienate and humanize the housing system, residents should be the primary decision-makers both in public and in private housing, and should have a stronger voice in the urban planning process.

Housing can be decommodified but democratized. The absence of tenant involvement in public housing management, or meaningless simulations of it, confirms the worst fears about public bureaucracies. In this respect, heavy-handed public housing administration plays directly into the hands of those who want to privatize all such dwellings.

When residents are included in housing management, too often it takes the form of meaningless consultations or ill-defined "involvement." But an angry tenant response to 1970s-era housing management reforms still holds: "Don't give me that

---

38 See Quintin Bradley, *The Tenants' Movement: Resident Involvement, Community Action and the Contentious Politics of Housing* (New York: Routledge, 2014); DeFilippis, *Unmaking Goliath*, 87–112.

participation bullshit, man. We want power!"[39] Too often, residential participation is empty theater performed by representatives of unaccountable managers. Instead, resident associations, tenant unions, community organizations, and households should be given actual democratic decision-making authority, as the true experts on their own housing.

What is true for the public sector is also true for private renters. The connection between landlord and tenant is as much a political relationship as it is an economic one. Private tenants should also have decision-making powers regarding the rules and conditions of their housing.

Again, some element of caution is needed. On its own, there is no guarantee that local decision-making is any more democratic or egalitarian than authority exercised at other scales.[40] Participants need to be sure not to reproduce domination at smaller scales. But the democratization of the housing system must be part of any solution to the housing problem properly understood.

Broaden housing struggles. Connect demands for radical housing policies to transformative demands in other areas. If oppression in housing directly intersects with other forms of oppression, then housing politics must intersect with other struggles. To succeed today, housing activists must find common ground with other social movements.[41]

---

39   Cited as a "folk saying" in Peter Marcuse, "Tenant Participation—For What?," Working Paper 112–20 (Washington, DC: Urban Institute, 1970), 1.

40   Mark Purcell, "Urban Democracy and the Local Trap," *Urban Studies* 43.11 (2006), 1921–41.

41   On housing social movements and the idea of the commons, see Stuart Hodkinson, "The Return of the Housing Question," *ephemera* 12.4 (2012), 423–44.

To be sure, housing activism has long been allied with other forms of social action. And activists rooted in non-housing movements have long raised important questions about residential oppression. For more than a century, feminists have argued that the house and home are prototypically political institutions, and have fought to transform them. Civil rights and antiracist activism has long seen housing discrimination and segregation as central to the struggle for racial justice. Alliances between these movements and housing activists are longstanding and should be strengthened.

Housing is a universal need that can take an infinite number of forms. Precisely for this reason, housing movements can potentially forge mutually supportive alliances with participants in a huge number of other struggles. The concerns of housing activists overlap not only with a variety of urban, anticapitalist, antiracist, and feminist movements, but also potentially with the environmental justice movement, the labor movement, LGBT movements, activism surrounding migrants' rights, disability rights, prison reform, community health, and many other sources of mobilization.

Democratize housing policy. That is, widen the process of decision-making on housing issues, and downsize the power of experts and bureaucrats. Housing is not a specialist concern, so it should not be the sole domain of specialists.[42] "Expose, propose, politicize!"[43] The housing system needs to be opened up to broader democratic

---

42 See Peter Marcuse, "The Pitfalls of Specialism: Special Groups and the General Problem of Housing," pp. 67–82 in Sara Rosenberry and Chester Hartman, eds, *Housing Issues in the 1990s* (Westport, CT: Praeger, 1989).

43 Peter Marcuse, "From Critical Urban Theory to the Right to the City," *CITY: Analysis of Urban Trends, Culture, Theory, Policy, Action* 13.2 (2009), 186.

scrutiny and input, so that it can be contested at a scale appropriate to its significance for everyday life.

Currently, the contours of the housing system are determined by a relatively small elite. As a result, the scale of inequality and injustice in the housing system is not widely acknowledged. We should not see these as unfortunate but random facts. That the basic shape of the housing system is not on any mainstream political agenda is a sign of the power of economic and political elites to make it seem as if fundamental housing questions are basically settled. We need to create new sites where the housing question can be reopened.

Many new housing developments are pushed through the planning process using arcane technical knowledge and backroom negotiations. The form and substance of this process needs to be changed. As the experiences of participatory budgeting in Porto Alegre, Belo Horizonte, and even New York City demonstrate, a more directly democratic planning process is possible.[44] Accounting measures should be used to reflect social priorities. The amounts of public subsidy given to any development project should be completely clear and open to public scrutiny. All viability assessments seen by any

---

44   Donata Secondo and Josh Lerner, "Participatory Budgeting Takes Root in New York City," *Social Policy* 41 (2011), 22–5; Gianpaolo Baiocchi, *Militants and Citizens: The Politics of Participatory Democracy in Porto Alegre* (Palo Alto, CA: Standford University Press, 2005); Yves Cabannes, "Participatory Budgeting: A Significant Contribution to Participatory Democracy," *Environment and Urbanization* 16.1 (2004), 27–46; Celina Souza, "Participatory Budgeting in Brazilian Cities: Limits and Possibilities in Building Democratic Institutions," *Environment and Urbanization* 13.1 (2001), 159–84.

government agency should be made public.[45] There should be social justice impact statements issued for all large-scale state and private actions affecting housing and land use, written in a way that the public can understand.

Planning today takes place in a technocratic language that excludes nonexperts. Most households are keenly aware of the nature of the housing crisis, but their perspectives are ignored by those who determine policies. In order to create a real right to housing for all, the epistemological basis of the housing system needs to be democratized.[46] The voices and experiences of poor households need to be central to the housing debate. There should be substantial amounts of financial and technical assistance to involve nonexpert publics in decision-making around community planning. A phrase that has long circulated in social movement circles should apply to the situation of poor and working-class households regarding housing policy: "nothing about us without us!"

Activists have long sought to contest the politics of housing knowledge, and plenty of groups pursue this strategy today. The Right to the City Alliance has held teach-ins, testified in hearings, and documented housing abuses across the country. The

---

45   For an account of how viability assessments are used to evade requirements to supply nonmarket-rate housing in the UK, see Oliver Wainright, "Revealed: How Developers Exploit Flawed Planning System to Minimise Affordable Housing," *The Guardian*, June 25, 2015.

46   Cf. David J. Madden, "There Is a Politics of Urban Knowledge Because Urban Knowledge Is Political: A Rejoinder to 'Debating Urban Studies in 23 Steps,'" *CITY: Analysis of Urban Trends, Culture, Theory, Policy, Action* 19.2–3 (2015): 297–302.

Anti-eviction Mapping Project has been documenting landlord abuse, displacement, and evictions, and collecting tenants' oral histories in San Francisco, Oakland, and elsewhere.[47] Housing experts have also worked to build similar alliances. Projects like the Planners Network in the United States or groups like Just Space and Architects for Social Housing in the United Kingdom try to place urban planning expertise in the service of progressive organizations and community groups.[48] Such alliances need to be expanded in order to combat the huge lobbying efforts of corporate landlords and developers.

The language of housing development needs to be contested and made less equivocal. Planners, architects, and others involved in housing and urban development need to actively refuse terms that muddle contentious political issues, and they should avoid technical or pleasant-sounding terms of art for actions that would be recognized as undesirable if properly named.[49] Phrases like "affordable housing" or "urban regeneration" are part of the process by which housing crisis and urban inequality are normalized. The language of housing needs to be repoliticized. We can start by refusing to engage in euphemism.

Globalize housing movements. Housing movements need to match the scale of the housing problem. Residential capital is

---

47 Emily Badger, "A Disturbing Animation of 15 Years of Evictions in San Francisco," *CityLab*, October 16, 2013. See antieviction.com.

48 On the question of "vanguardism" in such ventures, see Lily M. Hoffman, *The Politics of Knowledge: Activist Movements in Medicine and Planning* (Albany, NY: SUNY Press, 1989), 147–80.

49 See Peter Marcuse, "Blog #60. Toward a Housing Strategy for New York," *PMarcuse.wordpress.com*, December 17, 2014.

global in scope, with transnational investors and corporations determining the fate of households across the planet. Movements need to unite in order to address the problem at the same global scale.

Housing movements have long drawn on transnational connections. Early twentieth-century activists in New York City made use of immigrant social networks and experiences in European democratic politics. Their counterparts today have a similarly transnational orientation, utilizing cultural repertoires and political know-how from struggles in Latin America, East Asia, and elsewhere across the globe.

This cosmopolitanism is a resource that should be leveraged to address today's global housing crisis. Planet-spanning housing movements can help one another keep track of dispossession and displacement in different locations, identify strategic opportunities that might not be apparent on the local scale, share ideas, and foster worldwide public support. Such movements would resemble what the theorist Arjun Appadurai calls "deep democracy," a culture of solidarity without borders that enables those harmed by neoliberal globalization to respond at scale.[50]

Home, Not Real Estate

If a right to housing means anything, it must be the name of a movement to democratize, decommodify, and disalienate the housing system. The right to housing names a direction, not a

---

50 Arjun Appadurai, "Deep Democracy: Urban Governmentality and the Horizon of Politics," *Environment and Urbanization* 13.2 (2001), 23–43.

solution. The only solution is to struggle to make that right a reality.

Addressing residential injustice and inequality will demand state action as well as large-scale popular mobilization. A real right to housing implies radical social change. But a world where decent housing is provided to all is possible. It requires confronting the housing system without illusions and changing the processes that, generation after generation, produce residential and social crisis. The contemporary world already possesses the technical capacity and material resources to solve the housing problem. The question is whether all who are badly served by the status quo can unite to create a truly humane system, where housing is not real estate but is, instead, home.

Index

ABOUT GOLLANCZ

Gollancz is the oldest SF publishing imprint in the world. Since being founded in 1927 Gollancz has continued to publish a focused selection of bestselling and award-winning authors. The front-list includes **Ben Aaronovitch**, **Joe Abercrombie**, **Charlaine Harris**, **Joanne Harris**, **Joe Hill**, **Alastair Reynolds**, **Patrick Rothfuss**, **Nalini Singh** and **Brandon Sanderson**.

As one of the largest Science Fiction and Fantasy imprints in the UK it is no surprise we have one of the most extensive backlists in the world. Find high-quality SF on Gateway written by such authors as **Philip K. Dick**, **Ursula Le Guin**, **Connie Willis**, **Sir Arthur C. Clarke**, **Pat Cadigan**, **Michael Moorcock** and **George R.R. Martin**.

We also have a strand of publishing in translation, which includes French, Polish and Russian authors. Gollancz is home to more award-winning authors than any other imprint, with names including **Aliette de Bodard**, **M. John Harrison**, **Paul McAuley**, **Sarah Pinborough**, **Pierre Pevel**, **Justina Robson** and many more.

The SF Gateway
More than 3,000 classic, rare and previously out-of-print SF novels at your fingertips.
www.sfgateway.com

The Gollancz Blog
Bringing you news from our worlds to yours. Stories, interviews, articles and exclusive extracts just for you!
www.gollancz.co.uk

GOLLANCZ
LONDON